marketing methods to improve company strategy

applied tools and frameworks to improve a company's competitiveness using a network approach

marcos fava neves
luciano thomé e castro
matheus alberto cônsoli

Routledge
Taylor & Francis Group

NEW YORK AND LONDON

First published 2010
by Routledge
270 Madison Ave, New York, NY 10016

Simultaneously published in the UK
by Routledge
2 Park Square, Milton Park, Abingdon, Oxon OX14 4RN

Routledge is an imprint of the Taylor & Francis Group, an informa business

© 2010 Taylor & Francis

Typeset in Minion by HWA Text and Data Management, London
Printed and bound in the United States of America on acid-free paper by
Walsworth Publishing Company, Marceline, MO

Library of Congress Cataloging-in-Publication Data
Neves, Marcos Fava.
    Marketing methods to improve company strategy : applied tools and
    frameworks to improve a company's competitiveness using a network
    approach / Marcos Fava Neves, Luciano Thomé e Castro, Matheus Alberto
    Cônsoli. –1st ed.
        p. cm.
    Includes bibliographical references and index.
    1. Strategic planning. 2. Industrial management. 3. Marketing.
    4. Competition. I. Castro, Luciano Thomé e. II. Cônsoli, Matheus Alberto.
    III. Title.
    HD30.28.N4814 2009
    658.8′02–dc22   2009031116

ISBN10: 0-415-87375-4 (hbk)
ISBN10: 0-415-87377-0 (pbk)
ISBN10: 0-203-85986-3 (ebk)

ISBN13: 978-0-415-87375-8 (hbk)
ISBN13: 978-0-415-87377-2 (pbk)
ISBN13: 978-0-203-85986-5 (ebk)

Contents

List of Figures   vi
List of Tables   vii

Introduction   1

1 How to Describe the Company as an Integrated Network   4

2 How to Make a Strategic Marketing Plan Using a Collaborative Network Approach   16

3 How to Build Competitive Advantage through a Marketing Channel Plan   24

4 How to Analyze Channel Value Capture   37

5 How to Build and Review Marketing and Network Contracts   50

6 How to Build Competitive Advantage through Sales Force Planning   64

7 How to Strategically Build Joint Ventures   80

8 A Method for Building Competitive Advantage via Marketing Channels Incentives   91

9 Identifying Key Success Factors to Develop Market-Driven Strategies   101

Notes   111
References and Further Reading   113
Index   125

Figures

1.1 The company network 6
1.2 A wheat mill company's supply chain 9
1.3 The wheat mill company's marketing channels 10
1.4 The wheat mill network 14
2.1 Demand-driven orientation 17
2.2 Strategic and operational management 18
2.3 The proposed marketing planning sequence (framework) 19
2.4 The value chain 22
2.5 Potential inter-firm collaborative actions among business
     functions 23
3.1 A method for a distribution channel planning process 26
4.1 Marketing flows in the channels 40
6.1 Framework for sales planning and management 72
6.2 A template for remuneration plan 76
6.3 Increasing communication and information flows 77
7.1 A framework to build joint ventures 82
8.1 A sequence for designing incentives for distributors 93
9.1 Identifying key success factors 102
9.2 Example of key success factors for internal analysis based on
     competitors' reference 106

Tables

1.1 Marketing Flows and Company Activities   12
2.1 SMPM—Strategic Marketing Planning and Management
Process Under a Collaborative Network Approach   20
3.1 Flow Table   27
3.2 Possible Impacts of External Environment   28
3.3 Table of Impacts and Reactions   29
3.4 Power: Analysis of Channels Sources   30
3.5 Physical Specific Investment Analysis: Infrastructure and
Facilities   30
3.6 Table of Transaction Costs   31
3.7 Monitoring Activities, Company's Ability, Task Observability,
Cost   32
4.1 Comparison of Methods and Evaluation Systems in the
Studied Channels   42
4.2 Expressions to Calculate the Normative Participation in the
Channel Profits—Stage 1   44
4.3 Expressions to Calculate the Real Participation in the
Channel Profits—Stage 2   45
4.4 Expressions to Calculate the Real Participation in the
Channel Profits—Stage 3   46
5.1 Functions, Analysis of the Responsibility and Possible
Improvements   53
5.2 Asset Specificity Analysis: Physical, Technological,
Human and Brand   57
5.3 Specificity Analysis: Time and Location   58
5.4 Specificity Summary, Possible Risks and Contractual
Guarantees   58
5.5 Power Analysis   58
5.6 Summary of the Proposed Improvements   59

6.1 Overview of Selected Sales Planning and Management
Frameworks 67
6.2 Strategic Roles of Sales Person 73
6.3 Integrating Marketing and Sales Activities 74
6.4 Sales Objective Plan 74
6.5 A Realistic Analysis on the Best Sales Governance Method 76
6.6 Enhancing Communication Flows 77
7.1 List of Points to Discuss and Commit of the Previous
Relationship 83
7.2 Market Needs 84
7.3 Consolidated Chart of Companies' Core Competencies 85
7.4 Who Needs What from the Alliance? 86
7.5 Joint Venture Possible Advantages to Companies 87
7.6 Critical Success Factors—Conditions to Succeed for
Company C (Getting Over Disadvantages) 88
8.1 Objectives, Actual Situation and Performance Measures for
Activities related to Marketing Flows in Marketing Channels 96
8.2 Marketing Channel Benefit Packages 98
8.3 Creation of a Virtuous Cycle 98
9.1 Customer Wants Analysis 103
9.2 Company Resource and Capabilities to Overcome
Competitors 104
9.3 Relating Consumer Needs, Competitor Analysis and
Key Success Factors 105
9.4 Comparing Company and Competitors—Key Success
Factors (KSF) 105
9.5 Weakness and Strengths Related to Key Success Factors 107
9.6 Understanding the Link Between Strategy and the
Fundamental Orientation of Activities Within the Firm 108
9.7 Linking Strategy with Fundamental Competences Within
the Firm Using the 5 Forces Model 109

Introduction

This book consolidates ten years of work by the authors and brings together theory and methods that can be used for projects in both private and public sectors, and by academics in projects and research.

The book primarily intends to help practitioners and academics rethink business functions and gives them a clear guidance of how actually to do it. The chapters are written from a theoretical background and are formatted to enhance managers' ability to implement change.

The authors' experiences in implementing these ideas in organizations, and also by discussing them and consulting with executives in MBA classes, were fundamental to the creation of these methods. The central purpose of the book is to offer a managerial methodology—steps that can be applied to any firm in a logical and sequential manner.

Two central aspects are present throughout all the chapters. First, every method proposed has a strong market-driven philosophy. Each aims to align the firm to consumer needs, taking into consideration the position of competitors in the marketplace. We do more than just outline the theory, we want to show how it can be put in practice when working with, for instance, marketing and sales management. Second is the idea of the firm as a network. From the first chapter, where this concept is introduced, to the last, the network philosophy will reveal potential joint marketing activities, as well as joint ventures and other types of contracts and partnerships.

The first chapter discusses how to describe the company as a network. This is a basic tool in thinking strategically and forms a foundation for the following chapters. Where products and services are being bought and sold, visualizing the company as a network allows for potential partners and business models to be applied. It forms the initial chapter because simply looking at the the firm using this framework has frequently helped managers change their perspective and take different decisions.

The second chapter discusses the combination of marketing planning literature with a network perspective. It presents important innovations in marketing planning structures, and the reader is invited to think of potential joint marketing initiatives with other firms, such as competitors, in the network. Once again, more than just a theoretical discussion, this chapter shows steps managers can take to start the process.

Chapter 3 delves into the topic of marketing channels. Giving a more in-depth view of the firm downstream towards final consumers, it proposes steps to build competitive advantage through marketing channels. In a simple manner, it draws the attention of readers to the analysis of very important areas such as power, consumer channel services need, and gap analysis.

The fourth chapter deals with a challenge for marketing managers— distributing costs along value chains. Methods of estimating the share of work and costs in a chain of partner firms are clear, but managers must analyze any imbalances if the intention is to establish long-term relationships. The tool described in the chapter also helps to allocate actual and new roles to members in a value chain.

Chapter 5 deals with the very important, and frequently ignored, analysis of contracts with marketing partners. Once contracts are in place and firms are concentrating on their core business, partners have to be "governed" in such a way that value is preserved for the consumer. However, firms frequently take risks regarding committments made to partners and expose themselves, because of environmental change, to higher dependency. The tool in this chapter can be applied to help create safeguards.

The sixth chapter examines sales force management at a higher strategic level and, at the same time, intends to show operational implementation. The academic literature on sales is vast, and this area is a good example of where consolidation is needed to get theoretical and practical contributions framed in a manner which is useful for managers. What is new in the tool presented in this chapter is the opportunity to discuss the alignment of sales roles, environmental analysis, and compensation schemes.

Chapter 7 came about after analysis of two successful joint ventures and another that was not feasible. The chapter also includes subsequent improvements and evolutions of theory in this field. These allowed the creation of the method to help managers analyze and report on opportunities and threats that a joint venture may represent.

The eighth chapter includes a specific tool for aligning incentives in a supplier–distributor relationship. This is particularly important in markets where the distributor is fundamental in delivering information and services, as well as the products. The tool is designed to help create the best package for attracting and maintaining a motivated and aligned distribution network. In contrast to Chapter 5, where formal contracts are written and most probably enforced, this analysis is more internalised and manager-oriented. It assumes that relationships are more important than contracts and tries to introduce appropriate incentives for marketing channels.

Finally, the ninth chapter outlines a traditional analysis of critical success factors for a firm. We have tried to develop a tool which will facilitate managers in organizing market research or in brainstorming to create potential improvements. After using the tool, managers will have a clear idea of which areas to focus on using a market-driven philosophy.

The authors hope that after reading the book, managers will have a rich working agenda and that for academics, it will be useful in business colleges and MBA classes in providing a complementary theory with applied methods—something which students frequently ask for. At the end of each chapter there are questions intended to motivate readers to think about and implement the marketing and strategy methods presented in this book.

1

How to Describe the Company as an Integrated Network

After reading this chapter, you will be able to:

- Use the network approach to analyze business opportunities and threats of a particular company;
- Describe the network of a particular company;
- Think of joint initiatives a company might develop with several different business partners;
- Improve your analytical capability by understanding the network to which a particular company belongs.

Managerial applications:

- Improve marketing planning capabilities;
- Develop supply chain and distribution channel approaches to address marketing issues;
- Generate ideas for the creation of joint ventures;
- Redesign marketing channels;
- Redesign supply chain structures;
- Outsource business functions.

1.1 Introduction: The Importance of the Network Perspective

This chapter focuses on understanding how the network perspective may be used as a tool to help managers to think strategically. We offer a simple analytical tool to improve marketing thinking and create alternative actions which are capable of being implemented. First, the importance of the network perspective will be discussed and then the steps to undertake the proposed analysis will be described.

With the globalization of markets, firms and the marketing function have expanded their operations geographically. Outsourcing, partnerships, alliances and different business arrangements have therefore developed. In some cases, markets do not have boundaries and firms choose to specialize, demanding international contractual relationships, either to obtain their raw materials or to distribute their products and services. Real networks are being developed in order to focus on continuous and sustainable business relationships.

Several joint actions may be developed with different partners, whether it is with suppliers, distributors, competitors, indirect competitors, or service providers. Sometimes it becomes difficult to understand what is going on in a specific firm or a collection of firms. It is almost impossible to understand the strategic movement of these firms or the impact of analyzing them individually. To achieve a better business analysis, it is worth mapping and describing the network of companies involved in this venture.

Many joint actions are taking place in businesses involving supply chain activities and process integration. Groups of companies are coming together and are able to buy and sell more competitively. More and more firms are aware of potential gains of doing things together. This has become an enormous threat for any kind of intermediary in the market. Once firms cooperate flows of information are freely available, not to mention the information technology revolution caused by the Internet and electronic data exchange.

Cooperative marketing actions are receiving increasing attention and have been more and more supported by marketing executives and academics. Cooperation may be vertical in a network (between technologically distinct players, e.g.: suppliers and distributors), as well as horizontal, involving competitors and even firms offering complementary products to the same target market. These groupings help companies think differently, buy more efficiently, and market and cooperate more effectively. This may be achieved through potential logistic gains, communication actions or selling efforts..

These movements indicate that an analytical tool is needed to take a wider view of the firm, not limited to the firm's boundaries but including the group of businesses and the network within which they work. However, the methods of analysis already proposed in the marketing planning and control process literature do not have a strong network approach, but rather they consider the firm individually. As mentioned above, markets today are full of different partnering arrangements and these have to be considered strategically when preparing a marketing plan. Therefore we strongly believe that the network approach improves business options considerably.

Figure 1.1 illustrates a company network in general; understanding its elements and how they interact is fundamental to beginning an analysis of the network. The network's elements are the core company, the group of suppliers, the group of marketing channels, final consumers, facilitators, competitors, other networks and finally uncontrolled variables. They all interact to create value for the final consumer.

Here, it is important to focus on the network of members and the links between them. So, some structural aspects need to be considered when describing the network: a) the members of the network; b) the structural dimensions of the network; and c) the different types of links. The first assumes that members have some real importance in the network. These primary members are usually profit-making units, such as autonomous companies or strategic business units. The structural dimensions must take into account the horizontal structure (the number of tiers from suppliers to customers), the vertical structure (the number of members

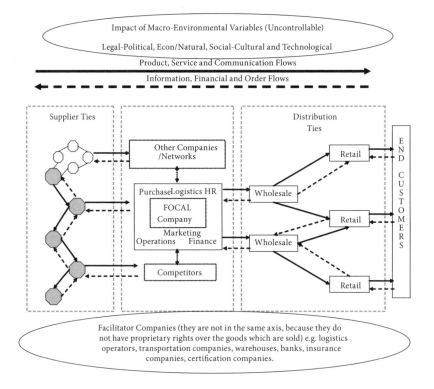

Figure 1.1 The company network

in the same tier) and the horizontal position of the core company. The types of links are related to managed process links, monitored process links, unmonitored process links and non-member process links.

To undertake a business analysis, such as the traditional macro-environmental (PEST—political, economic, socio-cultural, technological) analysis, it is necessary to be aware of every industry to which a core (or focal) company is related. An increase or decrease of input consumption of other networks might have a strong impact on the production costs of a focal company. The tool we propose here may increase the planning capability and creative solutions for the firm significantly.

The following steps must be taken to describe the company as a network:

1 Determine the focal company.
2 Identify the focal company's supply chain.
3 Identify the focal company's marketing channels.
4 Place facilitators in the network.
5 Place the competitors and other networks.
6 Develop a PEST analysis, deriving opportunities and threats for all the elements of the network.

These steps will be described below.

1.2 Determine the Focal Company

A network is comprised of companies that buy and sell goods and services, from the original raw materials through to when the goods reach consumers. Every company has a series of suppliers forming what is called the supply chain.[1]

At the same time, a company may have between itself and its final consumers a group of other companies, which form its marketing channels. The analysis depends on the focal company. Most of the time companies face challenges from competitors in buying the raw materials, as well as competitors buying or selling through the same or parallel supply chains and marketing channels.

Finally, facilitating the transactions between this sequence of companies there are several other firms, mainly service companies, which affect marketing flows. Marketing flows are the physical flow of products, service provision and communications going forward through the network, and the information, orders and financial flows coming backwards through the network. There is funding and risk sharing in both directions through the network.

By determining the focal company, its supply chain and marketing channels will be defined as a consequence. If the company is a food wholesaler, its marketing channels will be comprised of small food retailers, and its supply chain will be comprised of food industry firms. If the focal company is in the food industry, the food wholesaler is one of its marketing channels, and ingredients and raw materials suppliers are part of its supply chain. Once the focal company is determined, its supply chain can be mapped.

1.3 Identifying the Focal Company's Supply Chain

As we have briefly outlined, the supply chain is composed of the main suppliers of goods and raw materials and their suppliers. The criteria for including a company should be related to their relative importance for the final product. The question is: "who are the fundamental suppliers for the focal company?"

Obviously, the more suppliers in the supply chain, the more detailed the analysis can be, however this may reach an excessive level of detail, and will not useful for the analysis purposes.

When identifying the supply chain one could itemise all the inputs a firm needs for its production process. But the analysis here is different, since different inputs may come from the same individual supplier; all that is important here is to identify the supplier, not their particular inputs. In other words, this is not a representation of a production tree, but of the group of firms supplying the focal firm.

Figure 1.2 illustrates an example of supply chain for a wheat milling company.

Taking the milling company as the focal company, the figure shows the group of important suppliers. Understanding what is happening to them helps us understand what will happen to the focal company.

Sugar mills, salt producers and plastic suppliers are examples of important suppliers of wheat mills. But the most important supplier, the wheat producer, has its group of strategic suppliers as well, such as fertilizer, seed, agro-chemical and limestone suppliers.

Obviously, a long-run analysis of what is going to happen on the wheat seed market might indicate strategic movements for the wheat mill in its backward chain, as well as important developments for alternative international wheat suppliers in different parts of the world.

Fundamental questions to be asked at the identification stage of the analysis of the supply chain of the focal company are: "Which companies are my strategic suppliers?", "Which are the strategic

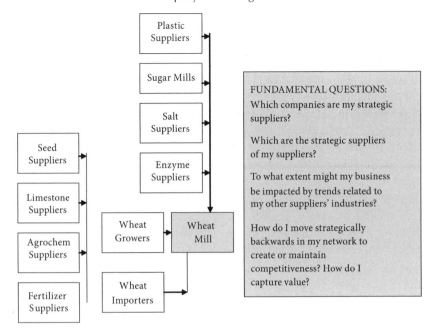

Figure 1.2 A wheat mill company's supply chain

Source: elaborated by the authors

suppliers of my suppliers?", "To what extent might my business be impacted by trends related to my other suppliers' industries?", and "How do I move strategically backwards in my network to create or maintain competitiveness?"

1.4 Identifying the Focal Company's Marketing Channels

Thinking of marketing channels, a company may reach the final consumer in several ways. Marketing channel literature defines the channel level as the numbers of intermediates between the focal company and the final consumer. Level 0 means no intermediary, Level 1 means one (probably a retailer), Level 2 means two (probably one wholesaler and one retailer), and so on.

Another aspect of analysis is the channel intensification. The company's marketing channel may be one of three levels: exclusive (only a few companies have the rights to trade products and normally this channel policy comes with territorial rights); selective, meaning the company uses a few distributors; and a mass channel policy, meaning the company will be happy to sell to any company which is interested in distributing the brand.

Practice has shown that for different product lines and market segments, companies use different channel levels and intensification policies. There is little sense in discussing one absolutely best marketing channel policy; in practice, the company has several channel options to reach the final consumer. A real network is formed. Multichannel policies have become the norm rather the exception in more and more fragmented markets.

Now, thinking of the channel options, let us use the same example to show how a wheat mill can place its products to reach the final consumer (Figure 1.3).

It should be noted that the value of companies in the marketing channels depends on the position of the focal company in the network. If, as in the example, a wheat mill is the focal company, firms in the pasta industry, baking industry and so on are channels for its products. It is also important to observe that the delineation of marketing channels of the focal company is independent of its product lines it sells. Certainly products sold to industrial clients are different from those sold to distributors, such as wholesalers and retailers, and different again from those sold to food service companies and bakeries. The analysis here is

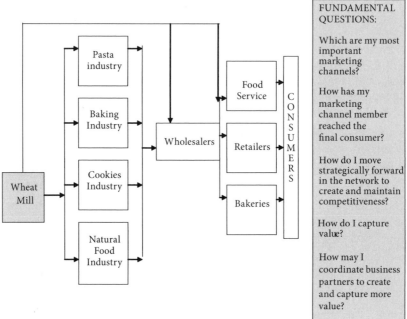

Figure 1.3 The wheat mill company's marketing channels

Source: elaborated by the authors

not focused on products sold in different channels. However, one may limit the scope if one was focusing on a specific product line.

Fundamental questions to be asked are: "Which are my most important marketing channels?", "How do my marketing channel members reach the final consumer?", "How do I move strategically forward in the network to create and maintain competitiveness?" and "How may I coordinate business partners to create and capture more value?"

1.5 Identify the Main Facilitators of the Network

This step will describe the firms responsible for performing product service, communications, finance, order and information flows activities which are necessary for networks to function and reach final consumers.

The firms which provide these services in the main stream of the network are known as facilitators; banks, logistic service providers, technical assistance providers, market research firms, communication agencies, and so on. Their services "facilitate" transactions in the network. This happens, for example, when a bank provides finance to a client to buy a product from a particular supplier, or when a communications firm helps to take the product's message to final consumers through a communication mix.

The purpose of this step is to describe all the agents that perform functions in the channel (part of the chain) for the company being analyzed. This allows us to obtain a more accurate view, understand the agents and analyze the functions they perform.

Table 1.1 lists the marketing flows for several activities in order to help managers identify who are the main facilitators present in a specific network.

In the wheat mill example important facilitators are: transport companies, communication agencies promoting the miller's brands, banks financing and facilitating wheat imports, and so on. The idea is to detail all service providers that matter. Opportunities and threats can also come from them.

1.6 Place the Competitors and Other Networks

Finally, it is important to place the main competitors in the network to understand if they just compete for the final consumer or if they compete also for your suppliers' capacity or for your distributors. Strategies to

Table 1.1 Marketing Flows and Company Activities

Function	Which Companies are Involved?
Product and Services Flow	
Inventory management	
Product transportation	
Product modification and after-sales service	
Customizing the product	
Providing technical service—support	
Product maintenance and repair	
Administration and handling of returned products	
Promoting product availability	
Providing other information to customers	
Packaging/specific packages requirement	
Evaluating new products	
After-sales follow up	
Industrial consumer services	
Keeping quality and others (fill in)	
Communications Flow (Forward)	
Sales promotion to final consumers	
Information about product features	
Advertising	
Providing sales force	
Measuring consumer satisfaction	
Frequent visits/ face-to-face contacts	
Packaging information	
Project tracebility requirement	
Website participation and others (fill in)	
Information Flow (Backwards)	
Sharing knowledge of local market	
Scanning data (access to computer data)	
Complaints via website/service line	
Electronic ordering	
Order frequency/formats consideration	
Consumer feedback and others (fill in)	
Payments and Financial Flows	
Conducting credit checks on final consumers	
Billing customers	
Caring for specific customer orders	
Arrange for credit provisions/financing	
Price guarantees and others (fill in)	

Source: elaborated by the authors using Corey et al. (1989); Rosenbloom (1999), Wilson & Vlosky, 1997; Jackson & d'Amico (1989) and interviews block competition and lock in clients and suppliers might be created with this first analysis when threats and opportunities are observed.

On the other hand, competitors may present opportunities for developing cooperative activities with gain for both parties, leaving competition to other levels. For instance firms may decide to cooperate on distribution and compete solely on brands, since availability will be equal.

Other networks may be related to the one being analyzed. For instance a wheat by-product may be an important raw material in another network. The development of this other network may increase the value of the wheat by-product and create alternative revenue streams for the company.

1.7 Once the Network is Described

Once the network is fully described, strategists may determine the trends related to external variables such as the political, economical, social and technological environments and their impact on the chain and consequently on the focal company.

An interesting example is the growth of the food service industry, caused by the growing importance of convenience and entertainment for the final consumer. This has a tremendous impact of how the wheat mill sells its products. Selling mainly to large supermarkets does not focus on this segment. Structuring channels to focus on food service companies might be a strategy to pursue.

The same sort of reasoning might be used to think backwards, forward and laterally. The idea is to broaden the analysis and enhance the capacity of managers to think of strategies taking into account the various firms that make up the business.

A final tool we propose is to think of political, economical, socio-cultural and technological trends which may impact firms in the network and consequently the focal company.

An interesting exercise is to think of trends related to the external environment and their impact on suppliers, marketing channels, competitors, facilitators, and finally for the focal company and to think of actions that may be taken by the focal company to exploit opportunities and avoid threats.

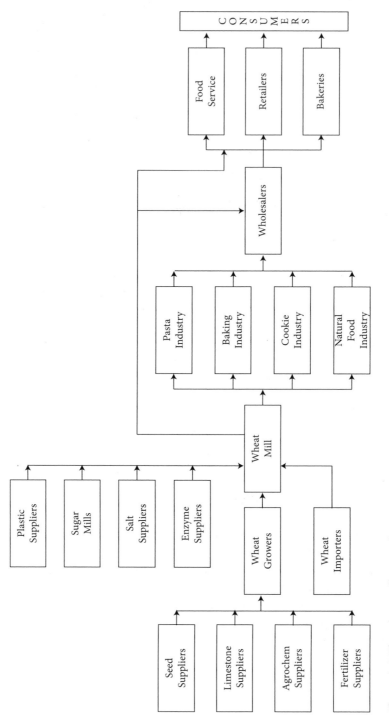

Figure 1.4 The wheat mill network

Source: elaborated by the authors

Summary

Marketing literature in general concentrates on the main sequences of marketing planning and control and does not have a strong network approach, but rather considers the company individually. This is a weakness of traditional marketing. There is a need to understand the company in a broader perspective: to view a company as more a nexus of agreements and contracts. To limit the analysis to the company as a sole unit of analysis might risk losing opportunities throughout the network to develop joint actions with firms backward, forward, and laterally. This chapter therefore demonstrates how to describe the company as a network. This was achieved with the following steps: first, selecting the focal company; second, describing its supply chain; third, describing its marketing channels; and finally describing important facilitators involved in performing marketing flows to aid the performance of the focal company network. This sequence has been applied and adjusted over several years, and it has been helpful in enhancing managers' capacity for understanding developments and their impact on the company in a holistic perspective. It forms a framework for idea creation and strategy generation—like focusing on the forest, and not on a particular tree.

Questions

1   Why does describing the company as a network improve the strategic planning capabilities of managers?
2   Think of a focal company and exercise the following steps:
   - Design the focal company's supply chain.
   - Design the focal company's marketing channels.
   - Place facilitators at the network.
   - Place competitors and other networks.
   - Develop a PEST analysis, deriving opportunities and threats for all the elements of the network.

2

How to Make a Strategic Marketing Plan Using a Collaborative Network Approach

After reading this chapter, you will be able to:

- Build and develop a marketing plan;
- Think of collaborative actions in marketing activities;
- Think of collaborative actions in other business functions in order to create and capture more value;
- Apply a particular method for creating and planning collective actions.

Applications:

- Marketing management;
- Strategic marketing analysis;
- Strategic alliances and partnerships.

2.1 Introduction: A Space for Adjustments in Marketing Planning Sequences

A review of academic marketing literature shows that the main methods of planning and control do not have a strong collaborative network approach, but rather consider each company individually. Most of them also have a more operational aspect and lack a strategic view.

The market has changed quite a bit in the last 20 years with the emergence of information technology, worldwide communication and information through the internet, specialization of competitors, global approaches, environmental regulations, changing consumer behaviors, and institutional changes. Companies had to face new and rapidly changing effects, and a change in management procedures had to follow.

Long-term planning seems static since environmental changes are faster than companies' adaptation capacity. To overcome these changes, academics and the private sector had to come up with a more strategic approach to management. The new way of thinking could be summed up in just two words: demand driven. As companies specialize, there is an increase in possibilities of partnerships, alliances and collaborative actions in order to take advantage of their core competencies.

A demand-driven firm considers the customer first, but at the same time, it does not lose sight of the competitor—an important benchmark. It means the company can build the best value plan for the customer and reach its desired profit level at the same time. If the firm is solely customer-oriented, there is the risk of creating disparity between what the customer needs and creating less value for the company, mainly because the firm creates costs rather than adds value. If a firm is solely competitor-oriented it is a risky strategy, because it runs the risk of becoming a follower. Figure 2.1 shows this schematically.

This figure shows that traditional approaches to planning processes are changed in order to adapt to the new scenario and prepare companies to reach sustainable growth. The major managerial implication of this chapter is to offer to practitioners in the private sector and to academics a new method for what we call "marketing planning." The demand-driven approach has seen an incredible growth in companies, and

Competitor Emphasis

	Minor	Major
Minor	Self-centred	Competitor-centred
Major	Customer-Centred	Demand/Market Driven

Customer Emphasis

Figure 2.1 Demand-driven orientation

Source: adapted from Gilligan (2003)

marketing planning has become more strategic, looking ahead. Since profit margins decreased in several industries, a more rational behavior in marketing was needed.

The difference between strategic management and operational management lies in the purpose of the analysis. Strategic management means defining the firm's direction and focus, while operational management means correctly implementing actions to achieve the strategic objectives. The same reasoning is applied to marketing, when it reaches a strategic role within today's markets. Figure 2.2 suggests two different dimensions in which to think about a firm's potential success: its strategic and operational effectiveness. The firm has to excel in both dimensions to reach a leader position in the chosen market.

After considering a demand-driven approach and the strategic role of marketing, it is important to understand that there are several activities in marketing that give scope for a *collaborative approach*, bringing a win-win situation for the companies involved. Companies are not isolated and in the new economy, take part in *flexible networks*.

This chapter presents a sequence of steps that was used as a strategic marketing planning and management (SMPM) process in several companies. It was built using case studies, extant literature, and focus groups. The SMPM method is new in that it views the company as part of a network (as detailed in Chapter 1) and makes use of inter-firm relationship tools.

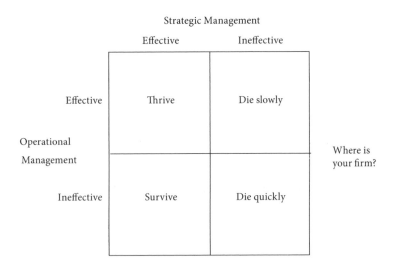

Figure 2.2 Strategic and operational management

Source: adapted from Gilligan (2003)

2.2 Steps for the Strategic Marketing Planning and Management (SMPM) Process

The steps for the SMPM process, as based on a collaborative and network approach are outlined in the framework below (Figure 2.3).

The proposed steps for the SMPM process are summarized in Table 2.1. This process should be done for a focal company, as illustrated in Figure 1.1.

It is important to mention that the strategic orientation of the plan is present from steps 1 to 5, where segmentation, target, and positioning strategies are defined, following the previous environmental, competitor and internal analysis. From steps 6 to 10, the traditional marketing variables are designed; these must be operationally effective. Steps 11 and 12 have to do with estimating the costs of implementing the suggested actions and guaranteeing they will be implemented and reviewed periodically.

Other traditional methodologies may be explored in order to think about the potential of collective actions to create and capture value. Let us make use of the value chain, from Michael Porter (Figure 2.4).

The chain is described as a set of primary activities directly related to the business function and support activities. Primary activities consist of supplier relationships (inbound logistics and operations)

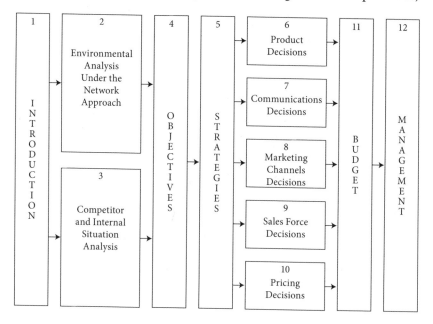

Figure 2.3 The proposed marketing planning sequence (framework)

Source: elaborated by the authors

Table 2.1 SMPM—Strategic Marketing Planning and Management Process Under a Collaborative Network Approach—Detailed Sequence of Steps

Steps	Summary of What Should Be Done
1. Introduction	• Make a brief history of the company and the alliances it has; • Verify whether the company has other plans already written and currently working; • Verify the compatibility of the marketing plan with other areas of the company (finance, operation, human resources, and production, among others); • Understand culture and teams that will be participating in the SMPM method.
2. Environmental Analysis under Network Concept	• Make detailed description of company's network (e.g. Figure 1.1); • Gather market data and conduct needed marketing research (external analysis); • Build general market analysis and trends; • Make a list of opportunities and threats ("step" analysis); • Describe and research consumer behavior (final and also intermediary customers); • Describe and research consumer (network) decision processes; • Evaluate and make a proposal for better functioning of information systems; • Elaborate a proactive list of collective actions in data generating and marketing/consumer research; • Make a budget for market analysis (budgeting of step 2).
3. Competitor and Internal Situation Analysis	• Develop competitor analysis and trends; • Compare the strengths and weaknesses of the company with those competitors; • Conduct benchmarking, based on competitors and from other firms of the network; • List possible collaborative actions for the reduction of weaknesses; • Establish benchmarking formal committees in the company.
4. Objectives	• List qualitative and quantitative objectives for the period of the plan (sales, market share, new markets, among others), normally for the next 3-5 years; • Include a high level of detail to allow the evaluation of goals; • Define key performance indicators and targets.
5. Main Strategies	• Consolidate the main strategies necessary to reach the objectives with a strong network and collaborative actions approach, that includes market segmentation, positioning, differentiation, products and services, communications, distribution, sales and pricing strategies; • It must be an answer to how the objectives will be accomplished; • This step is a summary of what is expected to be seen and detailed in steps 6 to 10.

6. Product and services	• Production facilities analysis;
	• Develop and improve technology;
	• Evaluate product line;
	• Launch of new products;
	• Offer new services;
	• Make brand decisions;
	• Make packaging decisions;
	• Use the concept of networks to verify the opportunities of partnerships (collective actions), like:
	  ◦ Bundling (complement product line with other companies' products);
	  ◦ Joint development of new products and innovation;
	  ◦ Development of markets and definition of dominant patterns;
	  ◦ Licensing of brands from other companies in non-competitive lines;
	  ◦ Share structure of packaging development;
	  ◦ Joint coordination of quality systems;
	  ◦ Share product recall projects.
	• Budget expenses related to the topics above.

7. Communications	• Determine target market(s) for communication activities;
	• Determine objectives to be reached at target market (s).
	• Define communication mix (advertising, sales promotion, publicity and public relations);
	• Identify possible partnerships for the proposed communication activities (collective actions), like:
	  ◦ Joint advertising;
	  ◦ Joint advertising for market growth as a whole even with competitors;
	  ◦ Joint sales promotion;
	  ◦ Public relations;
	  ◦ Development of lobbying;
	  ◦ Joint participation in fairs and events.
	• Define budgeting involving other members of the network;
	• Describe how evaluation (measuring results) of communications will be done and by whom.

8. Distribution Channels	
	• Analyze the channels and services provided (distribution flows);
	• Develop new channels;
	• Conduct asset specificity analysis and risk analysis;
	• Conduct channel benchmarking (competitors and other companies);
	• Conduct power analysis and conflict analysis for governance choices and decisions;
	• Conduct commercial policies analysis;
	• Conduct contractual analysis;
	• Initiate new partnerships in new and actual markets (nationally and internationally—see governance forms like franchise, joint-ventures);
	• Channel management: define the channel's functions regarding market information, product promotion, incentives for required actions;
	• Prepare channel budgeting;
	• Verify and describe how distribution activities can be done together by the network's firms for:
	○ Access to different market segments with complementary supplies;
	○ Strength channels of an individual company;
	○ Union of efforts from competitors to act in unknown markets;
	○ Blockage of distribution channels for competitors;
	○ Gains in economy of scale by better exploration of assets to the function of distribution;
	○ Joint distribution events;
	○ Joint investments (joint-ventures, franchise among other coordination forms).

9. Sales Force	
	• Determine current numbers and objectives for sales force;
	• Determine structure and strategy of sales;
	• Determine size and remuneration (commission policies);
	• Focus on performance: supervision, motivation and training;
	• Conduct evaluations;
	• Also propose activities that can be performed as collective actions, in cooperation with competitors and other companies that act in the same target markets, like:
	○ Share sales force (by companies with complementary products);
	○ Share sales representatives in non-explored markets (with competitors);
	○ Share training for salesmen (with non-competitors, with the same target market);
	○ Share customers database for visits (with non-competitors);
	○ Share information and to build a real business network (with facilitator companies—banks, insurance and transportation companies);
	○ Exchange information about market potential (with non-competitors);
	○ Offering a kit of products by salesman, becoming a real business consultant (with non-competitors products).
	• Budget for the sales force.
	• Define objectives related to pricing (maximization of profit, sales, market share, etc.);
	• Conduct demand analysis;
	• Determine production costs of company (by-product and product lines);
	• Analyze production costs and prices of competitors;
	• Determine method for pricing (mark-up and others);
	• Identify price variations, elasticity, patterns, and trends;
	• Define collaborative price strategies in the network of the company for:
	○ Buying both products (company A and B) and price reductions (special conditions);
	○ Increase the perceived value by customers;
	○ Reduction of the price elasticity in the attended segments;
	○ Reduction of costs;
	• Comparison among costs and competitors' prices.
	• Determine and consolidate expenses (investments) of steps number 2, 6, 7, 8, and 9.
	• The major decisions or strategies established should be transformed in projects, with a leader, a team, a budget, and deadlines;
	• In order for the SMPM method to be strategic, a strategy and marketing committee should be established. This committee will meet each month and evaluate the projects. There will be an agenda to present the projects and what was their evolution that month;
	• Every three months a longer meeting should be held where some of the tools presented in this book (and others that company chooses) could be discussed and applied;
	• Any impact from the business environment can create a new project to be inserted in the marketing plan;
	• Projects that are concluded or routine should then be eliminated from the strategic list, and new projects added according to market and competitor changes.

Source: based on personal application of marketing plans for 10 companies and suggestions from authors listed in references

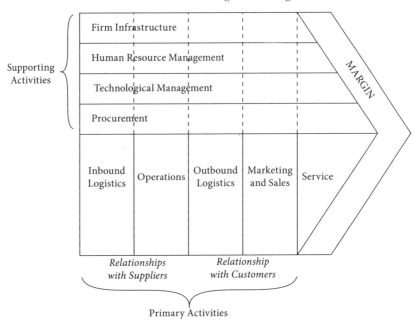

Figure 2.4 The value chain

Source: Porter (1980)

and buyer relationships (outbound logistics, marketing and sales, and service). Support activities consist of infrastructure, human resources management, the technology and purchasing departments.

The word chain is used because this is a sequential set of activities within a firm which creates costs but also adds value. It is critical that the firm is able to create more value at reduced costs in order to capture this value.

The word chain is also used because the chain may be extended to inter-firm collaboration. For instance, a wholesaler may work with a retailer to create more value for the final consumer. Therefore, it is possible to think of collaborative actions among business functions.

Figure 2.5 suggests some ideas of how to create work groups among firms, using Porter's framework.

To illustrate the usefulness of the method, workshops were developed with non-competing companies to generate marketing activities towards collaboration. This is explored in the next chapter.

Potential Differentiator at the Value Chain	Where advantage may be obtained?
• Physical Flow of Products among firms: Sales department with client's inbound logistics, Sales department with client's purchasing department. • Communication Flow: Marketing of both Companies. • Services flow: Marketing and operations of both Companies. • Financial Flow: Financial department of both companies. • Market Information: Marketing of both Companies.	• Reducing storage costs; • Shortening delivery time; • Potentializing better focusing communication actions; • Sharing services performance more efficiently among partners and consequently more satisfied clients; • Quickening product modification/adaptations; • Lowering costs of capital (the lowest costs are used in the chain); • More competitive prices.

Figure 2.5 Potential inter-firm collaborative actions among business functions

Source: authors, based on Porter (1980) and Arias & Akridge (2004)

Summary

Marketing literature shows that the main sequences of strategic marketing planning and control do not have a strong network approach, since these sequences consider the company individually. This chapter shows a sequence of steps, with a deeper analysis following in Chapter 3. What could be new, related to other planning proposals, is the idea of the firm in a network and the active use of inter-firm relationships and collective actions tools in marketing activities. Many collective actions may be done together by firms that operate in the same markets, whether they are competitors or have complementary products.

Questions

1 Think of potential collaborative actions that two different equipment suppliers (package and ingredients) for the beverage industries may develop and implement.
2 Using the value chain from Michael Porter, discuss how a supplier of agrochemicals can shorten the delivery time to an agrochemical dealer to improve its service level for growers.
3 Why would collaborative actions be difficult to implement in some cases? Think of at least three main barriers to implementation.
4 Use the method and build up a draft of a strategic marketing plan for a fictional company.

3

How to Build Competitive Advantage through a Marketing Channel Plan

After reading this chapter, you will be able to:

- Evaluate a firm's actual marketing channel strategy;
- Establish marketing channel objectives;
- Understand how to develop and implement a marketing channel plan;
- Monitor a firm's marketing channel strategy;
- Have an understanding of marketing channels, and apply theories such as transaction cost economics and relationship marketing.

Applications:

- Marketing channels and supply chain management;
- Strategic alliances with channel members;
- Marketing channels contracts.

3.1 Introduction

Many firms are unsatisfied with the distribution of their products and services. On the other hand, *distribution* channels, once strategically planned, may build stable competitive advantages, since they are designed and implemented over a long period of time, with a consistent structure, and are focused on people and relationships. This chapter presents a method to build competitive advantage through marketing channels, based on a sequence of steps to be implemented by marketers.

This sequence of marketing channel planning was elaborated based on the revision of four existing methods available in the literature,[1] and other contributions from supply chain management.[2] After this sequence was elaborated, it was submitted to ten marketing channel managers, who evaluated it and suggested contributions to be added in the proposed framework.

Before starting the description of the method, it is worth highlighting what is new about this method and how it contributes to existing ones.

- First, a sequence of steps was produced in which some tools from transaction cost economics (traditionally used in organization economics literature), not available in the other planning methods, are added to distribution channels planning.
- This sequence of steps may be more complete than other methods in the literature, because it combines more parts, it adds extra steps, and even adds more analysis to some steps based on contributions from articles and other sources.
- The method adds a step of power analysis, to help in the steps of building contracts, asset specificity analysis, and others.
- It considers as a first step an analysis of the whole supply chain and network, which is not suggested in the other distribution planning methods, which start by looking only at the channels (forward of the company).

Throughout the chapter, these characteristics will be detailed and their advantages will be made clearer for the reader. The chapter presents several charts and tables to be used by marketers interested in rethinking and redefining the firm's marketing channel structure.

3.2 The Description of the Method

This sequence can be organized in 11 steps ordered in four sequential phases (see Figure 3.1).

3.3 Detailing the Sequence of Steps

The next sections describe activities and analysis that must be performed in order to have a complete distribution channel planning process. The understanding phase starts with the description of the whole chain in which a firm is inserted, then the description of the marketing channels used by the firm being analyzed together with an environmental analysis.

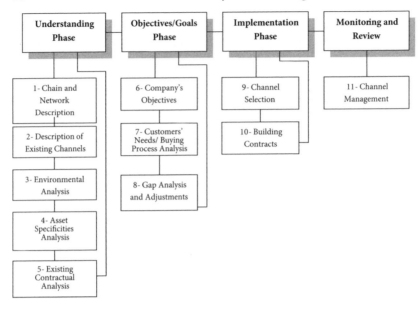

Figure 3.1 A method for a distribution channel planning process

Source: authors

Then, asset specificity analysis is done and the existing contracts are analyzed.

3.3.1 Description of the Whole Chain and Network

The purpose of the method is to describe, in a chart, all the agents that perform functions in the chain, from first suppliers to final customers, in order to have a general overview of the main companies operating in the chain, and, with this systemic approach, to make an analysis of the other chains that compete with the final product(s) (for details about how to describe the company network see Chapter 1).

If a company is operating in the poultry, red meat, sugar, orange juice, milk, or beer business, for example, just one system will be described. But for companies operating in more businesses, all the systems (chains) should be described, inserting the agents that perform negotiation functions (suppliers/raw material, farms, manufacturers, wholesalers, retailers, and others) at the product flow. With the recent trends of traceability (provenance), it is even more important to have this complete picture of the chain. This step will also add more insights to be discussed at the environmental analysis step.

3.3.2 Description of Distribution Channels of the Industry and of a Particular Company

The purpose of this step is to describe all the agents that perform functions in the channel (part of the chain) for the industry being analyzed. This allows for a more accurate view and understanding of the agents and for a first analysis of the functions they perform. An analysis of the consumption data, industry numbers, main companies, and other information should also be addressed at this step in order to facilitate and provide more information. After the aggregation level of the industry, the channels of the individual company should be described. The latter can be different from the industry channels, since some of these channels may not be in use. Sales and financial data should be provided in order to understand which channels are the most important for the companies' sales and profits. Table 3.1 can be used for each channel participant to document whether they perform the functions, whether they could perform the functions, and possible actions or improvements related to the function.

The following factors should be considered as functions, and one table for each of the flows could be built:

- *Product and services flow:* inventory management, product transportation, product modification, and after-sale service, customizing a product for the specific needs, providing technical service, product maintenance and repair, procedure and handling of returned products, promoting product availability, packaging, specific packaging requirements, evaluating new products, after-sales follow up, industrial consumer services, preserving quality, and others.
- *Communication flow* (from company to final customers): sales promotion to final consumers, information about product features, advertising, providing sales force, frequent visits/face-to-face contacts, packaging information, loyalty programs, website participation, traceability information, and others.

Table 3.1 Flow Table (one for each of the four flows)

Function	Actors	Alternative Solutions
...		

Source: elaborated by the authors using Corey et al. (1989); Rosenbloom (1999), Wilson & Vlosky, 1997; Jackson & d'Amico (1989) and authors' use in company projects

- *Information flow* (from customer to company): sharing knowledge of the local market, scanning data (access to computer data), complaints via website/service line, order frequency, order formats consideration, arrange information about consumption, and others.
- *Payments and financial flows*: conducting credit checks on final consumers, billing customers, caring for specific customer orders, arrange for credit provisions, price guarantees, financing, and others.

3.3.3 Environmental Analysis and Impacts to the Channel

Environmental uncertainties are unanticipated changes in circumstances surrounding an exchange. The greater the uncertainties, the higher the motivation for firms to seek governance structures that minimize transaction costs (Williamson, 1985). The purpose is to analyze some of the possible factors that could impact the industry's channels in the future and also the company's channels. The tool to be used here is the traditional "step" analysis, evaluating the socio-cultural, economic, technological, and political (institutional) factors. The step is well described in the literature (Johnson & Scholes, 1997; Mintzberg, 1994). Some insights to facilitate the specific analysis of drivers and implications regarding distribution channels are provided, using factors listed in literature and contributions from companies' managers (see Table 3.2).

- *Possible impacts of economic environment:* income changes, education/professional level, employment, exchange rates, interest rates, economic integration, supplier concentration, buyer concentration, business life cycles, GDP (gross domestic product) trends, capital and financial availability, inflation, energy availability, natural environment input constraints (water, air), tourism expenditure, and others.
- *Possible impacts of political/legal environment in the channels:* market access (protectionism), packaging recycling laws, anti-trust policies, economic integration (commercial blocks), labeling requirements, packaging constraints, types of communication constraints, tariffs

Table 3.2 Possible Impacts of External Environment

Drivers	Implications	Probability	Impact
...			

barriers, taxation policies, employment law, government stability, subsidy policies, product and/or process certification, and others.

- *Possible impacts of technological environment in the channels:* new technological solutions, mail sales, phone sales, internet sales, scanners, computerized stock, just-in-time deliveries, EDI (electronic data interchange), POS (points of sale) data, electronic funds transfer, automated ordering, technological transfer, ECR (efficient consumer response), VMI (vector-managed inventory), RFID (radio frequency identification, and others.
- *Possible impacts of socio-cultural environment:* women working, age demographics, race, time-reducing, elderly population, individuality, security, convenience, leisure, social mobility, income distribution, attitudes to work, lifestyle changes, family sizes, and others.

What actions should the company take if those listed factors happen? Table 3.3 can be filled in to obtain an overview of the process, which has the advantage of forcing the company to consider alternative plans to deal with environmental changes.

After the analysis of the environment, it is important to make a power analysis of the channel, power sources, and so on. This will bring about a better strategic understanding of the business, and of what the company should expect regarding negotiations, availability of channels, private labels, and other factors. Channel power refers to the ability of a channel member to control or influence the marketing strategy of an independent channel member at another level in the channel, possibly making them change their behavior, or perform an activity that they would not normally perform. The main sources are coercive power, reward power, referent power, expertise power, persuasion power, legitimate power, and information power (Lusch, 1976; Hunt & Nevin, 1974; El-Ansary & Stern, 1972). Moreover, it is interesting to understand the company's position in the chain and develop improvements (Slone, Mentzer & Dittmann, 2007).

Some tables regarding sources of power in the channels should be produced (see Table 3.4, for example), including their impact and how to deal with them in terms of possible best strategies to follow in order to reduce the power imbalance. The following method can be useful.

Table 3.3 Table of Impacts and Reactions

List of All High Impacts	Company/Channel/Chain Actions
...	

In it, the company evaluates power sources of the main agents that are used or will be used, for example, using a rating of 1–10 (very low to very high).

3.3.4 Asset Specificity Analysis

This analysis will be very important for building contracts and relationships, as it will provide insights into how to organize and coordinate the transactions in the channel. Anderson (1985) and John & Weitz (1988) state that there is a relationship between asset specificity and channel integration. The most important of these are physical-specific assets, time-specific assets, information and knowledge technology, human-specific assets, location (site) specificity, and marketing/transaction specificity. Filling in Table 3.5 can help in the analysis.

The following lists of factors were elaborated based on the literature[3] to illustrate specificities in marketing channels structures:

*   *Physical-specific investment analysis—Infrastructure and Facilities:* general factory, cold storage, special storage structure, tailored production facility, product demonstration facilities, specialized warehouses, repair and service centers, and other distribution channel investments.
*   *Time specificity analysis—refers to time pressure to do the transaction (flow):* shelf life (perishable), frequent/rapid deliveries, seasonality

Table 3.4 Power: Analysis of Channels Sources

Sources of power	Agent 01	Agent 02	Agent 03
Insert the source	Rating 1–10		
...			

Table 3.5 Physical Specific Investment Analysis: Infrastructure and Facilities

Type of Assets/Investments	Degree of Specificity	Reallocation Costs
	(High/Medium/Low)	(Impossible, High, Medium, Low)
...		

of production and consumption (inventory needs), and other time-related procedures.

- *Information and knowledge technology specific asset analysis:* EDI/equipment for electronic data exchange investments, software, management process by product category, joint logistic planning process, joint quality programs, traceability programs setting, new process joint generation, stock management process, and others.
- *Specific human asset analysis:* general training of distributors, joint sales training, production process knowledge, market knowledge, product brand knowledge, and others.
- *Site asset specificity analysis—refers to physical locations:* proximity needs (transport costs), energy supply, water supply, disposal of materials, strategic position of inventory, location of distribution centers, location of outlets (point specificity).
- *Marketing/transaction specific investments asset analysis:* conjoint brand development, joint planning advertising, packaging development, publicity efforts, and others.

Transaction costs are costs related to the occurrence of a transaction, or costs of governing the system (Klein et al., 1990), arising before and after the transaction takes place. These costs are normally not strongly considered in business analysis, but are very important in choosing strategies. Table 3.6 can help in this phase.

- *Ex-ante transaction costs:* price information search, product selling uncertainty, selection of alternatives, negotiation time, contract writing, search for quality information, search for buyers and sellers.
- *Ex-post transaction costs:* monitoring performance, redesigning contracts, renegotiations, monitoring property rights, monitoring technology copy, monitoring brand use, adaptation, legal disputes, non-delivery risks (supply), risk of losing contracts.

Table 3.6 Table of Transaction Costs: Possible Source of Transaction Costs in the Company's Distribution Channels, the Impact (High/Medium/Low) and How to Reduce it

Transaction Costs	Impact	How to Reduce Them?
(Types)		
...		

Additionally, Table 3.7 can be done individually for each channel in separate forms. Then a more specific analysis of ways to reduce transaction costs could be produced.

3.3.5 Existing Contractual Analysis and Benchmarking

Now it is important to understand how the relationships are governed in the distribution channels of the products in the industry, the coordination forms, general contract practices, and buying procedures/processes. It is important to decide whether the company is proposing, in the next steps, coordination forms that are very difficult to realize, and whether they will incur a lot of negotiation and learning costs. It is also important to understand and evaluate best practices.

The second phase deals with the set up of goals and objectives related to the firm's marketing channels. First the company's objectives are understood, and then customers' objectives and needs are analyzed. Finally, the method suggests a gap analysis and adjustments. These are the three next steps.

3.3.6 The Objectives of the Company

These should agree with the strategic planning program, if the company has one, or they should at least be consistent with the price, product, and communication strategies. The objectives (goals) should be set in relation to several variables, like volume ($), profit, sales margins, inventory turnover, market share, customer satisfaction, sales expenses, return on investment in channels, inventory expense, overall customer service level, volume (units) by product type, volume ($) per salesperson, volume ($) per quota, profit by supplier, volume ($) by product type, profit by product type, and others. In terms of behavior-based measures, the most important measures to be considered are

Table 3.7 Monitoring Activities, Company's Ability, Task Observability, Cost

List of Activities	Ability to Monitor	Observability of Activity	Cost of Monitoring
	High/Medium/Low	High/Medium/Low	High/Medium/Low
...			

service departments, warranty claims processing, building/facilities, office systems, employee incentive plans, coverage of trade area, product knowledge/salesperson, selling skills/salespeople, dealership financial plan, dealership business plan, advertising and promotion program, number of customer complaints, buyer credit management, sales forecast-accuracy, number of sales calls, calls to current customers, calls to non-customers, number of product demonstrations, and others. At this step, the company will produce several tables, forecasts, and other kinds of goal-setting tools.[4]

3.3.7 The Consumer's Objectives, Needs, and Buying Process

This step relates to marketing research with final consumers and intermediaries to gain insights about the perfect distribution systems from the consumers' point of view. The high cost of marketing research means that the kind of research that should be done depends on each company and their objectives; it is very important to build customer-driven distribution systems (Stern et al., 1996). According to Gattorna & Walters (1996), several methods are available to measure consumer satisfaction. First, in a design stage, it is important to establish the service and product expectations held by consumers. For this stage, a qualitative phase to generate a list of relevant service and product attributes based upon customer experience is interesting. This list will be used for the design of a questionnaire to be used in the quantitative phase.

All the functions and lists used in Step 3.2 can be used here to facilitate the understanding of consumer needs. Marketing research books (Malhotra, 1996; Hair et al., 1995; Aaker & Day, 1982) provide sufficient information and techniques. The buying process of clients and consumers must be considered and analyzed.

3.3.8 Gap Analysis and Quick Adjustments

The company has its own ideas about what it wants as a distribution channel and about consumers' desires, and at this step all these should be confronted in order to make the best feasible strategic decision for the company. All the goals should be confronted with market (consumer) restrictions and company restrictions. Quick adjustments refers to a step described in Stern et al. (1996) in which companies could get some insights from all the steps conducted so far and implement them immediately in existing channels, if they are clearly advantageous.

The third phase of the Method for Distribution Channels Planning Process is the channel election step followed by the construction of contracts and incentive systems with the chosen channel members. These two are described below.

3.3.9 Selection of Channels and Negotiation

Once the objective is set, the company can select the channel structure and channel members, if it has the flexibility to do so, which depends on the availability of agents in the channel, the kind of relationship that will be built, and several other factors analyzed in the preceding steps. For the negotiation process, several techniques are available, and a framework to build successful negotiations can be found in the work by Lynch (1993).

3.3.10 Building Contracts and Relationships

This step involves the design of written or other types of contracts (e.g. oral agreements) with the partners in the channels, or selling in market transactions or other forms, depending on the suggested coordination forms from the previous steps. Other aspects include contractual safeguards against opportunism in the channel, means of enforcement, adaptations to changed circumstances, building exit barriers, incentive design, and monitoring.

When creating contracts, participants must consider the possible conflict sources, establish ways to minimize these sources, and plan actions to be taken in case conflicts arise. If the company chooses a franchise format, it can find methods of contracts in the marketing channel books referenced above. If the company decides to enter a strategic alliance (joint venture) or other kind of relationship, Lynch (1993), Gattorna & Walters (1996), and the marketing channel references can be consulted for methods to be followed.

Finally, once everything is settled, the channel management comes as the fourth phase, as explained below.

3.3.11 Channel Management

The last step of the process is the management of the relationships. The literature on channel management is vast and it suggests several techniques and management skills. Only some aspects relating to building successful partnerships and trust, something of fundamental importance, will be highlighted here. The suggestion is to use references and tools of the relationship marketing, commitment and trust theory to help channels management (Morgan & Hunt, 1994). The physical process and logistics should also be strongly considered. Motivation of the members is an important task that the company should address

3.4 Final Comments

Finally, this Distribution Channels Planning Process should be done frequently to effectively address competitive advantages. The first time it is completed, the process will be time and money consuming, mainly for the companies that are starting from zero. However, once the process is done, the following analyses will be easier, because data are more organized and easily available, the knowledge of the planning process is known by the company and further decisions will consider what is new in the environment. Of course, not all companies where this sequence was applied completed all the steps presented here; some of the channels cannot be available (retailers, for instance), and for a company with several products, the analysis is more difficult, but extremely important due to the fact that distribution channels provide competitive advantage.

Summary

Research of existing literature reveals some methods (sequence of steps) for companies that want to plan distribution channels. None of these methods uses strong contributions from transaction cost economics, bringing a possibility to elaborate on a "distribution channels planning method," with these contributions and organizing the steps according to a sequence that would be useful for companies when reviewing the distribution process. This sequence was refined through in-depth interviews with companies. The method is composed of 11 steps organized in four different and sequential phases: the understanding phase, the objectives phase, the implementation phase, and finally, the monitoring and reviewing phase. Several graphs and tables are offered to the marketer to implement the method in his or her firm.

Questions

1   Give some examples of specific investments in marketing channels of a firm well known to you.
2   Show through an example how an environmental trend may impact a best channel design option.
3   What are, in your opinion, the critical organizational and human skills needed for channel management (Step 11)?
4   Choose a particular company and produce a draft of a marketing channels plans, using the method you learned in this chapter.

4

How to Analyze Channel Value Capture

After reading this chapter, you will be able to:

- Understand how value is created through a marketing channel structure;
- Understand how value is captured by different members in a given marketing channel structure;
- Rethink channel members' roles based in channel activities and value captured by them.

Applications:

- Marketing channels design;
- Marketing channels plan;
- Marketing channels power analysis;
- Competitive advantage created though marketing channels.

4.1 Introduction

A certain channel structure chosen by a particular firm is truly competitive if it creates more value than cost in the eyes of the final consumer, when compared with a competitor's channels structures.

It means that a firm should coordinate its efforts with channel members to create and capture value. However, to do so, several activities must be shared among channel members (we will call these marketing channel flows), as must costs and profits. How can we consider marketing channel activity in terms of coordination to value creation and profit sharing?

If there is a significant discrepancy related to value creation and value capture among channel members, there will be a long-term inconsistency in sustaining the competitive advantage created by the channel structure itself. For this reason it is important to understand who contributes what for the creation of value and how those contributors (channel members) are being rewarded by the existent channel margin system.

This chapter presents a method for evaluating the amount of work a channel member has in order to create the needed value in a certain marketing channel system and how it uses this value. More simply: "Does this reseller or manufacturer receive a fair amount of money, considering the amount of work it has employed to make these products competitive?"

Before explaining in detail the method for analyzing channel value capture it is crucial to gain a good understanding of fundamental concepts related to marketing channel design.

4.2 Fundamental Concepts

There are six groups of concepts which will be presented. Readers who are familiar with marketing channel literature may skip this section and go directly to 4.3.

The Systemic View and the Distribution Channels

Stern, El-Ansary & Coughlan (1996) comment that the distribution channels "...can be seen as a group of interdependent organizations involved in the process of putting these products and services to usage or consumption". Another important definition from the American Marketing Association considers them "an organized net (system) of agents and institutions which, combined, play all the necessary functions to connect the producers to the final consumers carrying out the marketing tasks".

Accordingly, the distribution channel is analyzed as an organized and complex structure that develops itself constantly. The channel is a dynamic system of specific marketing functions, not just a sequence of organizations involved in the distribution of goods (Dommermuth and Andersen, 1969).

Davidson (1970) comments that the distribution structure in the economy involves the retail institutions, lender services and wholesalers, as well as the producer's activities and the purchaser's efforts. Davidson also points out the importance of considering the producer and the consumer as active participants in the distribution process, especially in an era of integrated vertical systems that grow and share the marketing functions among levels of the distribution channels. According to Davidson (1970), several factors have contributed to the growing change in the distribution structures; those involve: (1) the accelerated growing of the marketing vertical systems; (2) the intensification of the inter-channel competition; (3) the rise in the polarity and concentration of the retail; (4) the acceleration of the institution lifecycles; (5) the emergence of the virtual corporations, very flexible organizations, with little fixed structure, with high use of the internet for connecting with partners, and flexible contractual arrangements with partnersinstead of employees; and (6) the expansion of retail "without stores."

The Importance of Channels and Intermediaries in Distribution

Alderson (1954), Stern et al. (1996), and Coughlan et al. (2002) point out the importance of the existence of channels, relating specific activities linked to the distribution function and attendance of the final users' needs, separating these reasons from demand and the supply.

From the demand side we look at factors such as: (a) the search facilitation, where the intermediaries help to reduce the uncertainties in the distribution process (necessity, market and transaction uncertainties) (Pelton, Strutton & Lumpkin, 1997) and (b) the adjustment of assortment discrepancies. From the supply side, what stands out are: (c) the creation of a routine transaction (d) the reduction in the number of contacts, and (e) the facilitation in the transmission and the exchange of information. In short, Coughlan et al. (2002) show that the intermediaries take part in the channel effort because they aggregate value and help reduce the channel costs.

"Services Production" by Marketing Channels and the Marketing Flows

A distribution channel can be seen as another "production line" engaged in producing not just the product that is sold, but also the complementary services, which define how this product is sold. These services, with aggregated value, created by the channel members and consumed by the final users, together with the product, are called "service productions". The production level of service includes breaking-bulk (breaking larger product quantities into smaller quantities according to consumer needs), space convenience, waiting time, selection, and variety (Bucklin, 1966; Coughlan et al., 2002).

Therefore, to satisfy the needs of the final users, the channel members carry out many functions to improve the level of service delivered to their clients. However, it is necessary that the channel members involved achieve good flow so that the correct level of channel services is reached.

Once the performance of the marketing flows is considered as an important variable of the analysis tool to the evaluation of the value capture in the channels, it is necessary to gain a wide understanding of its operation.

In a wide view, a useful way of "looking" at the distribution channels is evaluating what they do and how the work is done. The flows concept, which is related to the marketing functions, allows this visualization (Lewis, 1969). Figure 4.1 outlines a traditional distribution channel and its marketing flows. Understanding the marketing flows will play an important role, given that they are the basic variables of the proposed tool to analyze the channel capture value.

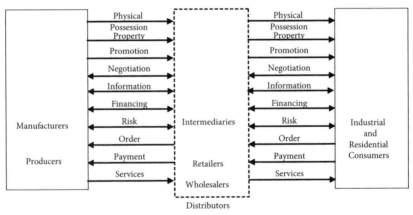

The dashed line in the intermediaries shows that the flows can be performed from the producer to the intermediary, from the intermediary to the consumer, from the producer to the consumer or shared among them.

Figure 4.1 Marketing flows in the channels

Source: elaborated from Rosenbloom (1999, p. 16) and Coughlan et al. (2002, p. 87)

Efficiency in the Distribution Channels

Coughlan et al. (2002, p. 93) state:

> Compensation in the channel system should be given on the basis of the degree of participation in the marketing flows and the value created by this participation. That is, compensation should mirror the normative profit shares for each channel member.

This subject, besides being related to the channel's efficiency, also relates itself to motivation questions and retention of channel members.

Pelton, Strutton & Lumpkin (1997) also deal with the equivalent subject as a way of relationship maintenance among channel members, and consider it as a fair and impartial distribution of the results. Jorgensen & Zaccour (2003) consider the profits' distribution as a coordination mechanism of channel members. To these authors, the profit distribution introduces a relationship between the total channel profit and the individual ones.

4.3 A Tool to Analyze Value Capture in the Distribution Channels

For the development and structure of a fee for the value capture analysis, a few methods, theories and systems were considered. They involve the planning, the structure analysis and the channel performance. It is important to point out that some of the methods, systems and analyzed stages do not have, as a main objective, the evaluation of the channel structure (see Table 4.1). This way, they were considered by being directly related to the proposed theme.[1]

The evaluation tool presented in this chapter is composed of the following aspects:

- The analysis of the importance of each channel flow to the supply of the demanded service level by the final consumer/user;
- The analysis of types and quantities of work carried out by each channel member in the channel flow performance and in the aggregated value by each channel member;
- The comparison of the participation resulted from the channel's total profits that each member must produce with their real participation in terms of gross percentages (real versus normative participation in the channel's profits);

Table 4.1 Comparison of Methods and Evaluation Systems in the Studied Channels

Theoretical Factors Pointed Out in the Methods	Contribution of Methods and Evaluation Systems in the Studied Channels as for the Selected Factors						
	Lewis (1968)	Bucklin (1973)	Hahn and Chang (1992)	Bucklin, Ramaswamy and Majumdar (1996)	Neves (1999)	Souza (2002)	Coughlan et al. (2002)
Main purpose of evaluation of flows' performance or services' level	No	No	Yes	Yes	No	No	Yes
Adjustment or choice's decisions of the channel's structure	Yes	No	Yes	Yes	Yes	Yes	Yes
Marketing flows' performance	Yes	Yes	Yes	No	Yes	No	Yes
Cost to perform marketing flows	Yes	Yes	Yes	Yes	No	No	Yes
Services' level to the final user	No	Yes	Yes	Yes	Yes	No	Yes
Identification/evaluation of conflicts' sources	No	Yes	Yes	No	Yes	Yes	Yes
Consider questions of dependence and power	No	Yes	Yes	No	Yes	Yes	No
Differentiate weights to flows or channel's services	No	No	Yes	Yes	No	No	Yes
Consider the question of aggregation value in the channels	No	No	No	No	Yes	Yes	Yes
Consider the profits' share among channel's members	No	Yes*	No	No	No	No	Yes**

* Consider the intermediary's profit given the control's level exercised by the producer;

** Consider the normative participation in the channel's profits, but do not mention or compare to the real participation.

Source: elaborated by the authors

- The support of the decision for the management and planning of the analyzed distribution channel.

It is proposed that the tool is detailed in three sequential steps:

1   Evaluation (Punctuation) of the marketing flows to the channel and the division of the activities among the channel members to calculate the normative participation in the channel's profits (Table 4.2);
2   Survey about the cost information and gross margin of the channel members to compare the real participation in the channel's profits with the normative one (Table 4.3); and
3   Analysis of the results and implications to the management and planning of the distribution channels.

The analysis of the results from the use of the proposed tool (Step 3) can contribute to many other stages of the channel planning method in Chapter 3: the channel description, the power analysis, existing contract analysis, analysis of the service level, and the consumers' needs, decisions of structure and adjustments in the channel, channel member selection, contract construction and channel management.

Following, in Tables 4.3 and 4.4, are the formulas and the methods for the first two stages.

Therefore, the proposed analysis tool can contribute to the channel managers' understanding about the current channel structure and the relationship of the companies with their partners, allowing correct actions to improve the distribution channels operation and performance.

4.4 Tool's Application

The channel value capture tool application must rely on managers' (mainly marketing, distribution, logistics, and sales areas) experience at identifying the contribution of flow performance, and knowledge of which members are carrying out these activities.

Table 4.4 shows the application of the channel value capture tool. The first activity that managers must discuss is the weight that each marketing flow in the channel will take. It is not monetary information, but it must reflect the managers' opinion about which marketing flows are more "expensive" for the channel and those that are not. This analysis must be done in the way that weight sum is 100. The second column of Table 4.4 presents an example of this analysis.

Table 4.2 Expressions to Calculate the Normative Participation in the Channel Profits—Stage 1

(a)

$$\sum_{i=1}^{n} CF_i = 100\% \quad (1)$$

where

CF_i = Weight of total cost of the i flow,

(b)

Let

CFa_i = Weight of adjusted cost of the i flow,

PB_i = Benefit potential of the i flow, and,

$$-1 < PB \leq 1$$

Consider that,

If the i flow presents high potential of benefit,

$$PB_i > 0;$$

If the i flow presents medium potential of benefit,

$$PB_i = 0;$$

If the i flow presents low potential of benefit, $PB_i < 0$;

$$CFa_i = \frac{\left[CF_i \times (1 + PB_i) \right]}{\sum_{i=1}^{n} \left[CF_i \times (1 + PB_i) \right]} \quad (2)$$

(c)

And so

DP_{ij} = Proportional performance of the i flow by the channel member j

so,

$$\sum_{j=1}^{n} DPij = 100\% \quad (3)$$

where $\begin{cases} i > 0, e \\ j \geq 0 \end{cases}$

Therefore

$$\sum_{i,j=1}^{n} \left[CFa_i \times DP_{ij} \right] \div 100 = PN_j \quad (4)$$

where

PN_j = Normative participation of the channel member j.

(d)

And

$$\sum_{j=1}^{n} PN_j = 100\% \quad (5)$$

For

j_1 = First channel member (producer),

j_2 = Second channel member (intermediaries),

...

j_n = Last channel member (final consumer).

Source: elaborated by the authors

The second step is the identification of the benefits potential for each marketing flow to the channel performance. It is an important definition, because a high-cost flow does not denote a high-benefit one. For example, imagine a retailer that distributes refrigerators. It is a product with high storage costs, because it takes a lot of space and volume in a warehouse and the benefit potential is low, because few customers are used to buying and transporting a refrigerator on their own.

Table 4.3 Expressions to Calculate the Real Participation in the Channel Profits—Stage 2

(a) Let	c) So,

(a) Let

$$LB_j = \left[\left(C_{j+1} \right) - \left(C_j \right) \right] \qquad (1)$$

where

LB_j = Gross profit of the channel member j,

C_j = the products' cost for the channel member j,

$C_j + 1$ = the products' cost for the channel member j immediately right.

(b) And let

$$PR_j = LB_j \div LC \qquad (2)$$

where

LC = Gross profit of the channel,

C_{jn} = Last channel member (final consumer),

C_{j1} = First channel member (producer).

c) So,

$$LC = C_{jn} - C_{j1} = \sum_{j=1}^{n} LB_j \qquad (3)$$

where

PR_j = Real participation of the j member in the gross profit of the channel.

(d) And,

$$\sum_{j=1}^{n} PR_j = 100\% \qquad (4)$$

Source: elaborated by the authors

We suggest that analysts assign higher benefit potential to those flows which are very important to channel performance and customer added value; and reduce it for those flows with lower importance, as exemplified in the third column of Table 4.4. The next column is the final (adjusted) cost weight of the marketing flows.

The next activity that managers must complete is to define the participation of each channel member in the performance of the marketing flows. Analysts must rely on managers' experience and figure out the amount of work necessary to perform all activities related to a specific flow that is performed by each member. In the previous example, a manager's opinion is that from the activities related to the product (warehousing, transport, etc.) 35 percent is performed by the company that produces the product, 35 percent by the wholesaler who first distributes the product, 22 percent by the retailer that sells to the final consumer, and 8 percent by the consumer, who buys the product, transports and stores it in their house. The same must be done for all marketing flows, remembering that the sum of each member performance must be 100.

After these activities it is possible to calculate the normative participation of the members in channel performance. It is a weighted average that expresses the proportional job that each member, including

Table 4.4 Expressions to Calculate the Real Participation in the Channel Profits—Stage 3

	Weights for the flows			Proportional flows' performance to the channel members				
	Costs %	Benefit potential	Final weight	1-Manufacturer	2-Wholesale	3-Retail	4-Consumer (final user)	Total
Products	18	1.60	22.36	35	35	22	8	100
Promotion	20	1.50	23.29	30	30	35	5	100
Services	15	1.50	17.47	30	40	30	0	100
Negotiation	8	1.10	6.83	20	50	30	0	100
Financing	6	1.00	4.66	35	30	15	20	100
Risks	5	0.70	2.72	45	30	20	5	100
Information	8	1.00	6.21	50	30	20	0	100
Orders	12	1.10	10.25	30	40	25	5	100
Payments	8	1.00	6.21	35	45	20	0	100
TOTAL	100	–	100	–	–	–	–	–
Normative participation in the profits (%)	–	–	–	32.63	36.19	26.65	4.53	100

	Cost Member 1	Cost Member 2	Cost Member 3	Sales' price to the consumer	Total
	100	120	162	210	
Costs' analysis/ members' share	20	42	48	–	110
Real participation in the profits (%)	18.18	38.18	43.64		

Source: elaborated by the authors

the final consumer, is performing to add value through the channel. Coughlan et al. (2004) define the normative participation as the share that each member should be proportionally receiving from the total channel profit, although it is well known that value capture in channels is not always proportional to the performance of the marketing flow.

In this way, the proposed tool seeks to help managers to identify these differences and develop actions to increase the channel performance, better distribute activities among members, and reduce potential conflicts. This analysis involves identifying the product cost for each member. In the example (Table 4.4) the product cost was 100 to the manufacturer, and it was sold at 120 to the wholesaler, that sold at 162 to the retailer, and so on. The gross margin for the producer was 20, for the wholesaler was 42 and the retailer got 48. The total channel "profit" or value added was 110.

Finally, the channel analyst can calculate the "real profit" participation of each member and compare it with the normative participation. In the previous example, the manufacturer profit share was 18.18 (20/110), but its normative participation was 32.63! It shows that the producer is not capturing value compatible with the marketing flows performance. On the other hand, for the retailer (in the example), profit share (43.64) is higher than the normative performance (26.65), highlighting that this member is able to capture value in a better way than other channel members.

The objective of the value capture tool is to support managerial decisions about channel management. Its use can help managers understand problems and opportunities in the channels they use to distribute their products. Moreover, it presents powerful information for decision making and problem solution. At least some adjustments must be done to reduce the negative impacts of remuneration misbalance among members.

Furthermore, several actions and decisions can be incrementally applied to improve channel structure, reduce conflicts, increase members' commitment, reduce channel costs, and booster competitiveness and channel future performance.

4.5 Final Considerations and Managerial Implications

It can be pointed out that the channel value capture tool deals in its analysis with the main decision areas which involve the channel management, such as strategy questions, structure, some selection and motivation factors, strategic coordination of channel members, performance evaluation, and conflict management (Mehta, Dubinsky & Anderson, 2002, p. 430). It can help in the planning, management, and decision making by the channel managers, if they follow the proposed stages which offer: (1) better understanding of the company's distribution channel, of its members, and above all, of the channel service orders by the final users; (2) evaluation of which members have larger activity loads in the marketing flows, while revealing how the costs are shared among the channel members; (3) contributions of each channel member for the value creation in the channel, while also allowing an important analysis of each marketing flow to the channel performance; and (4) a structured analysis of possible opportunities, adjustments, and improvement actions that can be done for the benefit of the distribution channel and the company.

This way, the tool can be used by the company to evaluate the existing channels, as well as to stimulate the development of new channels and serve as an instrument of comparison among the various channels used by the company.

Summary

A certain channel structure chosen by a particular firm is truly competitive if it creates more value than cost in the eyes of the final consumer, when compared with competitors' channel structures. It means that a firm should coordinate its efforts with channel members to create and capture value. However, to do so, several activities must be shared among channel members (we will call these activities marketing channel flows), as well as costs and profits. How can we consider marketing channel activity coordination in relation to value creation and profit sharing? The proposed tool consists of three steps: (1) Evaluating the marketing flows to the channel and the division of the activities among the channel members to calculate the normative participation in the channel profits; (2) Survey the cost information and gross margins of the channel members to compare the real participation in the channel's profits with the normative; and (3) Analysis of the results and implications to the management and planning of the distribution channels.

Questions

1   Choose a particular firm that employs channel members in its distribution efforts and calculate the normative margins the channel members have in the system.
2   Do you think the normative numbers are different from the real numbers? What are your reasons?
3   Use the framework to analyze margins and services performed in a channel.

5

How to Build and Review Marketing and Network Contracts

After reading this chapter, you will be able to:

- Understand what is truly going on in a certain marketing contract;
- Understand what clauses should (or should not) be inserted in a marketing contract;
- Analyze risks in marketing transactions and how these risks can be mitigated;
- Understand how asset specificities play a major role in defining one's position and possible strategies;

Applications:

- Outsourcing marketing functions;
- Reviewing marketing contracts with suppliers and distributors;
- Define and review sales representatives contracts.

5.1 Introduction: Why Marketing and Network Contracts?

Changes in the economic environment have increased the need for companies to focus their activities in their core competencies and outsource others, thereby reducing diversification levels. In this context, the vertical integration (realization of distinctive technological phases under the same decision command) frees space for inter-organizational contracts as an alternative coordination structure (relationships). The so-called "hybrid forms" gain space in the world of governance relationships. Since hybrid forms are mostly done by contracts, the importance of the training process for building, analyzing and revising contracts is clear and of growing importance in business management.

Contracts are elaborated in a changed environment and in the presence of bounded rationality. Bounded rationality is defined as the inability to foresee ex-ante, in other words, before the beginning of the transaction of future eventualities.[1] Incomplete contracts can lead to problems and bring undesirable transaction costs that could be reduced if the process of building a contract included more detail. This chapter describes an exercise that has been successfully used as a tool to analyze contracts and to propose improvements in networks.

5.2 The Method for Contracts Analysis in Networks

> If contracts give rise to problems…why have them? Contracts, whether implicit or explicit, involve some kind of continuing relationships between two or more parties. There are simple contracts such as "I agree today to buy your house tomorrow"…The contracts I'm interested are both more durable and more complex.
> (Stiglitz, 1992, p. 293)

Contracts from a wide range of sectors were analyzed to produce this managerial tool: a supermarket and a dairy products supplier, an animal health product supplier and the sales force, a clothing company and its retailers in shopping malls, a vehicle industry and its authorized dealers, orange growers and processing industries and several others over four years of use and improvement.

To understand the general functioning of the method, a contract between companies might be chosen. The contract is then analyzed using the following methodology: (1) Drawing the company network and understanding the contract and group discussion; (2) the responsibilities in the contract in relation to marketing flows; (3) asset specificity analysis and risk analysis; (4) analyses of possible control sources (power); and (5) contract improvements (suggestions) and institutional considerations. These steps will be detailed in the following sections.

5.2.1 Drawing the Company Network, Understanding the Contract and Group Discussion

In the first step, you should draw the company network that has the contract being analyzed (see examples in Table 5.1). Then, study the document and present interesting topics about the document, the company, and finally which transaction the contract is governing (controlling) in that particular company network. The design of the network should follow the instructions given in Chapter 1.

5.2.2 The Responsibilities in the Contract Regarding Marketing Flows

The second step will study which responsibilities the contract brings in relation to product flow, services, communication, financial, and other information necessary for the functioning of the transaction and to reach final consumers. Chapter 4 discussed in detail the work related to marketing flows in order to create and capture value.

As an example, Table 5.1 refers to the traditional marketing channel flows by inserting or deleting points according to the analyzed contract. To use Table 5.1, fill in who does what action and how in the middle column; the right column follows possible improvements.

After filling in Table 5.1, several discussions about how the company and its counterparts are developing the existent flows will be done looking forward to a series of contractual improvement suggestions. The right column of the table can be enhanced to list improvements with responsible people, goals, and deadlines.

5.2.3 Asset Specificity Analysis and Risk Analysis

The asset specificity refers to how much the investment (asset) is specific for another use (Williamson, 1985); that is related to the loss of the asset value in a second best alternative (Klein et al., 1990). According to Bello & Lohtia (1995), investments that are bound to an exchange relationship cannot be put to an alternate use. Azevedo (1996) defines how the assets are put to use unless with value loss. Once the assets are specific and hard to allocate for other relationships, the guarantee against agents' opportunistic attitudes should be in the contract (John 1984).

There are six types of specificities involving the transaction. First we should see which assets are involved and which ones have been considered.[2]

Specificities arise according to the transactions among different participants in a network. From buying inputs, processing, marketing and delivering, the different participants interact in a dynamic network of contracts and relationships. Some parties may be more

Table 5.1 Functions, Analysis of the Responsibility and Possible Improvements

Function	Analysis of the Responsibility (who does what and how)	Possible Improvements for the Contract
Product and Services Flow Variables		
Management and inventory levels		
Product transportation		
Product modification		
Product line and variety		
Evaluation of new products		
Predicted volume of sales (performance)		
Technical support of explanation/installation		
After-sales service		
Providing of sales (team) service		
Training: scope and costs		
Maintenance and product repair		
Packaging subjects/specifications		
Brand subjects		
Exclusivity details found in the contract		
Territorial rights found in the contract		
Predictable market coverage		
Duration (period to perform the flows)		
Adaptation to specific laws		
Others (fill in)		
Communications Flow Variables		
Advertisement (all forms)		
Sales promotion (all)		
Public relations actions (all)		
Direct marketing actions		
Providing information about products		
Sharing in communications budget		
Communication within direct sales		
Packaging information		
Others (fill in)		
Information Flow Variables		
Providing information about consumer's market		
Providing information about competitors		
Providing info. about changes in the environment		
Participation in the planning process		
Frequency and quality in information		
Providing complaints information		
Electronic orders		
Others (fill in)		
Payments and Orders Flows		
Order frequency		
Pricing policies and payments		

Continued …

Function	Analysis of the Responsibility (who does what and how)	Possible Improvements for the Contract
Margins analysis		
Commissions (volume and frequency)		
Conducting credits to final consumers		
Billing customers		
Search for financing sources		
Pricing guarantees		
Others (fill in)		

Source: elaborated by the authors

or less exposed to opportunistic behaviors depending on the level of specific investments they have made.

Considering a transaction between a yogurt producer and a supermarket, several assets are involved to make this transaction successful: the yogurt production industrial unit, transportation companies, retailers, human resources, technology, brand and the yogurt product. Next, to facilitate the analysis, we should classify the types of assets involved generally and give examples:

Dedicated or physical specificity: this analysis refers to the assets involved in the production of the product. For example, orange juice extractors, sugar cane mills, beer factory fermentation machines, citrus orchard, are specific investments for the related activities; reallocation is practically impossible in some cases resulting only in their recycling/ scrap costs. Anderson & Gatignon (1986) cite the example of specific machines acquired: printing, packaging, development of specific packages for the product, factories, specific storage systems (cold), special storage structure, services, and repair centers. Also included are investments made by the producers in the distribution channels like special displays, refrigerators, coffee machines, and others.

Specificity connected to human resources: this specificity is related to human resources of the companies directly or indirectly involved in the transactions; for example a highly specialized employee trained in technology, knowledge of the market (group of customers), suppliers, distributor training and sales training. Those human assets can be drafted in the market or trained in the company; they represent a cost in which his or her reallocation for another activity, depending on the specificity, is nearly impossible without losses.

Technological specificity: the company, in order to make a transaction, invests in a technological process that is sophisticated and specific, and it is an investment of high reallocation costs. There are processes of fermentation, food preservation (irradiation), new molecule production, new specific action principles to yogurt culture, etc.

Brand specificity (marketing): this specificity is linked to the building of a name, a brand, the reputation in a certain market, the effort of public relations within the community, with the press, developing packaging, etc. It can also include the efforts of communication predicted in the contract in order to make a positioning of a certain product, advertisements, activities for sales promotion, and others. Sometimes the reallocation of a brand to another product may be impossible.

Local (site) specificity: the assets involved in this transaction have local restrictions due to the characteristics of transportation of the product, for they should be close in order to successfully perform the transaction. For example, a wheat mill sited in Brazil can use Canadian, Argentinean, Asian, or Brazilian wheat, whereas a refinery cannot count on sugar cane produced in Thailand or in Cuba for its supply. In the supermarket example, regarding transactions of products like beer, milk, and mineral water among others there is a greater local specificity involved in the buying of alkaline batteries or powdered juice among others. Other possible local specificities involve the need of proximity to a natural resource (water), energy (gas pipelines), raw material, strategic positions of warehouses and distribution centers and certain specificities linked to commercial sites (shops).

Time specificity: this specificity refers to the time spent on the performance of the transaction. The analysis is focused more on the product and takes into consideration two major factors: its perishable characteristics, and its storage policy. Products such as farm produce have a high time specificity. The supermarket has bigger difficulties in the supply of produce from farming than their transactions of buying canned products, for example. The greater the time specificity, the subtler the transaction and also the smaller the universe of alternatives. Other examples include the need for fast and frequent delivery due to "just in time" policies, among others.

Usually, this is the most difficult part of the method because most of the time it deals with a new form of analysis for managers. Table 5.2 is a starting point for this analysis. To fill this in, find factors of specificity in the transaction (considering all assets listed above), fill in the second column (the asset owner), then fill in the third column if the specificity is considered high, medium, or low, and finally fill in the last column if there are alternative uses.

Time and local specificity analysis is considered separately, since they do not involve an owner; they refer to specific characteristics of products or asset locations involved in the transactions. Table 5.3 is a starting point for this analysis. The contract analyst must identify and indicate in the middle column any specificity factors found in the transaction. Additionally, in the right column, the analyst can analyze the risks involved in the transaction, evaluating if they are high, medium or low risk.

How can this analysis be useful to recall, improve or even build a contract? With the transactions and specific assets based on Tables 5.1 to 5.3, a summary of where specificity problems arise can be made. If there are possible actions to reduce problems (such as new or alternative uses for the specific assets), they should be selected to try to reduce the risk of opportunistic behavior from the other party.

What are the risks involved and what types of contractual guarantees should be considered based on this specificity analysis? Table 5.4 presents a suggestion of how to organize a risk and contractual guarantees analysis, which is central for this method, and a summary of Tables 5.2 and 5.3.

5.2.4 Analyses of Possible Control Sources (Power)

In establishing a contract between companies, another important analysis is the possible power sources that a company has and how they could be used in an agreement.[3] It is useful for the company, based on power sources, to build an analysis involving the company and the contract partner. The following method can be used where an evaluation of the company's own power sources and those related to the contract partner are, for example, ranging from 0–10. In Appendix 1, a Table with the main power sources is provided.

To fill in Table 5.5 analyze the existing power sources in Appendix 1. A source is inserted in the left column and a score is given from 0 to 10 based on the magnitude of the source for each party involved in the contract. Later, in the right column possible ideas should be thought of to reduce this imbalance.

5.2.5 Contract Improvements (Suggestions) and Institutional Considerations

At this moment several improvements to the contract, or its next version, can be made. They can be ordered by importance and should also be considered as possible wishes of the partners and for future

Table 5.2 Asset Specificity Analysis: Physical, Technological, Human and Brand

Type of Asset Investments	Asset Owner	Degree of Specificity (High/ Medium/Low)	Reallocation Costs
Alternative Uses (Impossible, High, Medium, Low)			
Physical Specificity			
Factory			
Cold storage facilities			
Special storage structure			
Tailored production facilities			
Product demonstration facilities			
Repair and service centers			
Distribution channels investments			
Others			
Technology Specificity			
EDI/equipment for electronic data exchange			
Sharing process of logistic planning			
Joint process of logistic planning			
Joint quality programs			
Tracking/tracing programs			
Software investments for supply			
Others			
Human Specificity			
General training of distributors			
Joint sales training			
Production process knowledge			
Market knowledge			
Product & brand knowledge			
Others			
Brand Specificity			
Joint brand development			
Joint planning advertising			
Packaging development			
Sales promotion development			
Public relations development			
Others			

Source: authors

Table 5.3 Specificity Analysis: Time and Location

Type of Specificity	Possible Presence	Degree of Specificity (High/Medium/Low)
Time Specificity		
Expiry date (perishable)		
Frequent/rapid deliveries		
Seasonality of production (inventory needs)		
Seasonality of consumption (inventory needs)		
Other		
Location Specificity		
Proximity needs (transport costs)		
Energy supply		
Water supply		
Availability of materials		
Strategic position of storage		
Location of distribution centers		
Location of outlets (point specificity)		
Others		

Source: authors

Table 5.4 Specificity Summary, Possible Risks and Contractual Guarantees

List of All Assets of High Specificity	Risk	Contractual Guarantees

Source: authors

Table 5.5 Power Analysis

Power Source	Company	Another Company of the Contract	Contractual Forms to Reduce Power Imbalance
Insert the source	Score 0–10	Score 0–10	Insert here

Source: authors

conflict sources. This could be interesting for the companies to prepare themselves before the transaction process starts. The marketing proposals for contract improvements (e.g. commitment to advertise, sales agreements, commitment from the sales force to share information) should take into account the country's laws; check if it is possible in that particular environment to propose such improvement, that is if it does not interfere with the local regulations. Specialist lawyers could contribute to this analysis.

Thus, a large summary table should be made (Table 5.6) with the factors taken from the right columns of Tables 5.1, 5.4 (which is the combined summary of Tables 5. 2 and 5. 3) and 5.5.

5.3 Final Comments

At the moment of elaborating and proposing improvements in a contract, a suggestion to monitor and control could be a reward mechanism that motivates each party to honor contractual clauses. This way, incentive systems would entirely or partially substitute the inspection and punishing mechanisms. The contractual hold-up is not desirable in the majority of the cases. According to North (1990) in Zylbersztajn (1995), there are factors that lead to an automatic enforcement of contractual clauses with fewer hold-up risks, including reputation, the company brand, the so-called "social network" and the loss it will have in the market if it does not meet the agreement.

It is important to say that this exercise (method) is improved each time the process is used. The discussions and group work are exciting and productive. It is also a tool for students and managers in the training for contracts and how to work with lawyers. The companies with their contracts analyzed had, as a consequence, new suggestions

Table 5.6 Summary of the Proposed Improvements

Proposed Improvements	Implementation Probability (Legal Aspect)	Partner Expected Reaction	Techniques for Negotiation and Stimulus
Insert the listed factors from right columns of tables 5.1, 5.4 and 5.5.	Insert if there is legal restriction for such improvement	Insert if this will be a factor with easy, moderate or difficult acceptance	Insert what will be done to stimulate the partner to accept the change

Source: authors

for the improvement of the instruments (contracts). The executives that participated also had a satisfactory impression about the discussions.

In the network economy, the process of building more complete contracts is very useful. This chapter brought some contributions to help the process of building or reviewing contracts from the company.

Summary

Bounded rationality makes it almost impossible to build complete contracts to manage transactions between companies. Furthermore, incomplete contracts generate opportunism problems from one of the involved parties and undesirable transaction costs that could be reduced if the process of building a contract were to be done with more detail. In general, business people do not have the instruments to facilitate this process of building, and students, who will deal with contracts in various moments of their professional lives, are not trained for this activity. This chapter provides a method that has been successfully used as a contract analysis tool in business networks focusing on marketing actions. The contract is then analyzed using the following methodology: (1) drawing of the company network, understanding of the contract and group discussion, (2) the responsibilities in the contract in relation to marketing flows, (3) asset specificity analysis and risk analysis, (4) analyses of possible control sources (power) and (5) contract improvements (suggestions) and institutional considerations.

Questions

1 Choose a firm and a particular contract with an organization where you believe the relationship might improve by using the proposed tool to enhance the governance mechanism (contract) and review the responsibilities in the contracts and asset specificity and risk analysis.

2 In the same firm, are there other relationships without formal written contracts that could be subjected to the same analysis?

3 Which are the most outsourced marketing functions nowadays? Are they all subjected to the same contractual analysis? How do they differ regarding the types of contracts?

Appendix 1 Power Source in a Channel (Systems), what they Refer to and Examples

Power	What They Refer To	Some Examples/Channels	Problems
Coercive power (use is negative)	• Threatening procedure due to the capacity of a member to punish another. It is based on the magnitude of the punishment and the credibility of the threatening message if the threatened member perceives that the costs in not agreeing are higher than the costs in agreeing.	• Discontinuing sales to a distributor who has weak service performance or gives discounts or unauthorized prices. • Refusing to deal. • Threatening to discontinue due to unauthorized use of suppliers. • Threatening to introduce vertical integration. • Forcing full line products. • Adding another distributor to the area. • Allowing direct sales (or via web) • Motivating channels via "black" markets.	• Continuous use leads to legal problems. • Generating associations to countervail. • Enhancing the level of conflicts in the channel. • Reducing information exchange incentives. • High costs and risks of losing the network or the supplier. • Reducing of inclination to long term relationships.
Reward power (use is positive)	• Possible rewards to members contribute to establish power and to work as established.	• Compensating sales force. • Offering of price discounts due to performance. • Offering guarantee of goods supply in shortage.	• It can be difficult to distinguish between this and the coercion depending on the way it was used. • It can be limited to the geographic area or availability of "rewards". • Notice the offer as an indication of weak performance. • Diminishing returns: agents get used to new patterns.
Reference power (use is positive)	• Company image or successful brands contribute to this power. There is a desire to be identified with this member of the channel.	• Establishing strong brand. • Have national or global presence. • Create store loyalty. • Create own brand loyalty.	• Losing trust in cases of wrong uses of image and brand.
Expertise power (use is positive)	• Use of knowledge in operation systems, such as market knowledge, knowledge in promotion techniques at sales points and others.	• Creating high economy of scale. • Creating cost structure of business. • Having training and learning skills. • Having site location knowledge.	• Losing trust in cases of mistakes made in knowledge and suggestions given through this.
Persuasion power (use is positive)	• Rational appeal based on size, financial position, knowledge and concentration. It is not threats, but its role as leader. • Offering large discounts to gain bid or orders. • Having shelf space. • Sharing market. • Centralizing purchasing. • Charging for space.	• Ethical problems. • Legal problems.	

Power	What They Refer To	Some Examples/Channels	Problems
Legitimate power (use is positive or negative)	• Guaranteed by contract; there is knowledge on behalf of the channel that power exists.	• Using franchising and other contract forms.	• Problems in thinking that previous vertical structures behave the same as the contractual structure. • All incomplete contract problems.
Information power	• Data about costs, sales and prices used to influence the negotiation.	• All sources of information that propose asymmetry and advantages. • Examples: scanned data.	• Can be restricted to this ability and may not be sustainable. • Ethical problems and difficulties in building strong relationships.

Source: authors based on several interviews

6

How to Build Competitive Advantage through Sales Force Planning

After reading this chapter, you will be able to:

- Identify the critical roles your sales team may play to create competitive advantage;
- Think of aligned policies to sustain the sales strategy regarding an incentive system, sales structure, and governance mode, among other sales decisions;
- Understand how to implement new sales strategies;
- Reflect on marketing integration as focused on sales management.

Applications:

- Sales planning and management;
- Quota systems and compensation;
- Sales training and motivation;
- Sales control.

6.1 Introduction

Sales literature could be grouped into five main topics. First, introductory themes deal with the sales tasks and classification, the new role of the salesperson, buying behavior, and the sales process.[1]

The second topic and one which has been explored in-depth by researchers is sales organization. It includes the choice between employed salespersons and independent representatives, setting the size of the sales force, territory alignment, the alignment between marketing strategy and sales strategy, the establishment of the organizational structure and level of centralization, the sales manager role, account management and the determination of sales quotas for the level of specialization of the sales force.[2]

The third topic is human resources in sales. These are policies and actions related to acquiring and maintaining a well-prepared and motivated sales team, including recruiting and selection procedures, training, motivation, and compensation. The fourth is related to sales control and auditing. Finally, the fifth discusses sales automation and information technology.[3]

Although the sales literature is vast and complete, and advances have been made, the frameworks for the sales planning and management focus on only one aspect or another and may also lack managerial orientation towards an organized framework for sales managers. A framework is supposed to organize in a logical sequence the actions which must be undertaken by sales managers. It also shows the relationships between the decisions. Besides, a particular industry may require decisions which are not taken into consideration or which are only briefly treated by general frameworks.

There is an increasing demand for services and a better qualified sales team, the increasing concentration among clients, leading to increased buying power and emergence of key accounts, the existence of sales and marketing channels conflicts, the internationalization of the sector, and the coexistence of several different formats of salespeople (as employed, distributors, agents, independent representatives, and independent consultants). Hence, the new and complex business environment is a fertile ground for updating and adapting these general frameworks.

The central objective of this chapter is to propose a sequence of steps for sales planning and management that consolidates the existing sales literature and covers the critical aspects brought by the new business environment.

The objectives mentioned above are reached by comparing the existing frameworks for sales planning and management to the critical aspects regarding today's sales management. The existing frameworks are selected according to their importance, as identified by the frequency of citation by sales researchers, or simply they are from traditional sales authors. The chosen ones are Churchill et al. (2000), Ingram & LaForge (1992), Dalrymple & Cron (1995), Ryans & Weinberg (1981) and Chonko et al. (1992).

To understand how the proposed method was created, it is useful to go through sections 6.2 and 6.3 where some existent frameworks were analyzed and then some gaps with evidentiary demands from marketing managers were brought for discussion and insertion in a new sales planning framework.

6.2 Most Used Frameworks for Sales Planning and Management

Table 6.1 shows five classical sales planning and management frameworks and their main group of activities. The extreme left column tries to group common steps suggested by the authors and the numbers in the columns below author names is the original order proposed by them.

The Churchill et al. (2000) framework is one of the more classic ones. It is composed of environmental analysis, the marketing strategy definition (regarding the design of the marketing mix), and the sales management activities which include account management, sales organization, sales planning, sales deployment, supervision, recruitment, selection, and motivation. The next phase is the understanding of the determinants of the role perceived by the salesperson, which is defined by the sales management activities and also the external environment. The perceived role, together with the firm's sales activities will define the salesperson's performance. This performance can be then evaluated and give feedback to the marketing planning process to restart the process. Although complete, the present framework does focus the role perceived by the salesperson and his or her performance. Also, important sales organization decisions are grouped together. Finally, it appears not to guide sales management decisions.

The framework developed by Ingram & LaForge (1992) is composed of six steps. First the authors suggest that the company and the sales managers must develop a complete understanding of the sales activity to enable them to properly manage the salespeople. Then the sales strategy is defined, which includes the definition of relationship strategies, or what level of relationship will be pursued by the salespeople with different clients, and also a channel strategy which means multiple channel choice. Sales organization tasks are related to sales organization topics and the sales force development and direction to the topics on human resources in sales. Finally, the determination of sales force efficacy and performance is related to the process of demand estimation, quota determination, sales budgets and evaluation procedures. This is also a broad and complete framework with additional aspects when compared to Churchill et al. (2000), since it includes the definition of relationship strategies and the multiple channel management.

Table 6.1 Overview of Selected Sales Planning and Management Frameworks

Common suggested Steps	Churchill et al.	Ingram and La Forge	Dalrymple and Cron	Ryans and Weinberg	Chonko et al.
Environmental analysis and business planning	1.Environmental analysis		1.Business Planning	1. Environmental analysis	1. Environmental analysis
Marketing Planning	2. Marketing strategy definition		2.Marketing Planning	2.Marketing strategy and action plans	2. Marketing Planning
Sales Planning (and sales organization decisions)	3. Sales management activities definition	2. Sales strategy definition 3. Sales organization design	3. Sales Planning	3. Definition of the desired personal selling role 4. Sales Organization policies and procedures	3. Sales Planning
Salesman Perceived Role	4.Understanding of the salesmen performance determinants	1. Complete understanding of the sales force function			
Topics in Human resources in Sales		4. Sales force development Sales force Guiding		5. Territorial Sales Manager Implementation	4. Sales Staffing Implementation of sales activities
The Sales Process				6. Interaction buyer-seller	
Results	5.Results		4. Results on profit and customer satisfaction	7. Results	
Control	6.Sales Control		5. Sales Evaluation		5. Sales Control
Feedback		5. Determination of sales force efficacy and performance	6. Feedback on Performance		

Source: elaborated by the authors based on Churchill et al. (2000), Ingram and LaForge (1992), Dalrymple and Cron (1995), Ryans and Weinberg (1981) and Chonko et al. (1992)

Dalrymple & Cron (1995) provide a method with the first three steps composed of business, marketing, and sales planning as the traditional marketing planning literature suggests. The sales plan is composed first of market access, definition of client relationships and operational budget, and then by targeting, sales force organization, demand estimation, territory design, and topics on human resources. Then these plans will lead to results on sales, profits, and consumer satisfaction. The sales evaluation is done followed by the feedback provided to resume the process. Among all frameworks, this is maybe the most straightforward one.

Ryans & Weinberg (1981) presented a framework published in their article entitled "Sales force management: integrating research advances" which, although rather old, among the frameworks analyzed is the only one published as a paper and not as the introduction of a sales management textbook. First the authors describe the interaction between the strategic, tactical, and operational levels, in which policies are implemented from the top to the bottom and information on results goes the other way. The framework starts with an internal and external situational analysis, then the definition of the marketing strategy and action plans follow. The sales planning is divided into three levels: sales organization policies and procedures (which would be the strategic level), then the territorial sales manager implementation (the tactical level, which means that the sales manager has to implement regionally what has been defined strategically), and finally the interaction between buyer and seller (the operational level, where there is a sales process that may build satisfactory results).

Finally, the framework from Chonko et al. (1992) presents a sequence composed of environmental analysis, marketing, and sales planning. This last one contains sales organization issues, the establishment of sales objectives, and sales plans. Next, staffing considers the decisions of human resources on sales. Additionally, the authors suggest an implementation phase composed of motivation, compensation, sales support, communication mechanisms, and delegation referring to the role of the sales manager. Finally, as a last step control activities are suggested including the design of report systems, performance standards, performance evaluation, and corrective actions.

6.3 What is Missing on the Sales Planning Methods?

6.3.1. Gap 1

Information and communication management regarding the salespeople, territorial sales managers, and the firm: several companies show dissatisfaction with the distance between salespeople, sales managers, and the firm. It is a general feeling that the firms have grown, advanced to new regions—nationally and internationally. Some common problems are: We feel that we could better explore the information on market developments, new product opportunities, and competitor actions coming from our salespeople; How could we improve information exchange among representatives?; I feel my salespeople are far away from the firm...How can my territorial sales managers function as a bridge between the firm and the salespeople and the market?

Information management from the market to the firm is well discussed in the marketing literature, more specifically in marketing information systems and marketing research. Aside from Chonko et al. (1992), none of the analyzed frameworks inserts the design of information and communication flows, which can be worthy to add.

6.3.2 Gap 2

Conflict management: most companies show conflicts related to the use of multiple marketing channels; more specifically on direct sales and among representatives or salespeople related to territory invasion. These lead to several problems of marketing channel efficiency. In other words, the integration between the direct sales force and the marketing channels used are crucial and may deserve more emphasis. The marketing channel literature has discussed these conflicts, ways of conflict minimization, and resolution (Geysks et al., 1999, Friedman & Furey, 1999, Brown & Day, 1981, Rosenbloom, 1973) and authors in sales have also discussed the conflict risks of using several different formats (Zoltners et al., 2001).

6.3.3 Gap 3

Territorial and other sales policies: A lot of time has been invested by firms discussing the rules for selling across territories. What are the conditions where one salesperson can sell to another territory, considering possible exceptions like new clients? What happens if a client wishes to be served by another representative and not the original one from the territory? Some answers given when asking representatives about their satisfaction with the firm indicate the importance of this topic: The company should pay commission to the representatives from the territory from every sale done in the region, and it does not!; I feel other dealers and the firm's direct salespeople are competitors, the company should make the rules clear in the territory and not leave us to cope with such unstable and critical issues!

Although the sales literature has discussed specialization of salespeople, once a choice is made (for territories, clients, products, sales process, or hybrid structure) more issues are definitely left to be solved and the quoted frameworks do not mention them.

6.3.4 Gap 4

Definition of the sales manager's role: firms have shown strong dissatisfaction regarding the sales manager's role. What are the major sales manager's responsibilities, considering the tasks of sales management? One thought is: Managing a sales team is different from what we have. Our sales managers spend too much time selling and management tasks are left unsolved.

Different authors have analyzed the sales manager's function (e.g. Ingram et al., 2002, Futrell, 2003) and the methods of Dalrymple and Cron (1995), Chonko et al. (1992) and Ryans and Weinberg (1981) have also mentioned it. However, the responsibilities between sales management, territorial sales managers and salespeople in territory management have not been made clear by the frameworks.

6.3.5 Gap 5

The choice between representatives and employed salespeople: although the sales literature has shown the importance of this decision and its relationships with other decisions—like those on compensation and control, and even on sales implementation (Albers, 2000b)—general frameworks simply group it together with sales organization decisions. The make-or-buy decision in sales may deserve more emphasis and, in a sequential decision set, it could be positioned as one of the first choices a firm makes, considering all the analysis recommended by transaction cost economy and agency theory (Anderson & Weitz, 1986, Albers, 2000b). This decision has also been shown by Zoltners et al. (2001) in their go-to-market strategies as one of the very first steps in sales planning, after the market segmentation and the understanding of the critical work is needed by each market segment.

6.3.6 Gap 6

Recommendation for the management of representatives: once the choice for sales representatives has been made, several other important issues may emerge. Much time has been invested by firms in representatives' contract construction and revision for companies, and alternative practices to try to avoid the pitfalls of using representatives. Chapter 5 presented a framework for building and reviewing marketing contracts. Moreover, ways to manage an outsourced marketing function has been shown to be an interesting research topic (Anderson & Weitz, 1986). Therefore, it might be interesting to add steps of sales representatives' management in a sales management framework, when using them.

6.3.7 Gap 7

Strategic and operational integration of sales with other marketing variables: as with other marketing variables, sales have to be integrated into the marketing mix. Our experience with firms shows how critical this aspect is to the firm's performance. General frameworks have just mentioned this need when discussing marketing planning, but the marketing literature has discussed the authority salespeople may have on pricing and its effects on profitability, channel integration (discussed in Gap 1), and the integrated communication plan. Also, the idea of the salespeople as service provider shows the integration between the offer (or product mix) and the sales function. Some guidelines are needed to show how to integrate the sales function into the marketing mix.

6.3.8 Gap 8

Collective sales forces and support: we have seen the importance of marketing joint actions once firms build competitive networks. Opportunities for collective actions in the sales area are also increasing due to small marketing budgets. Moreover, consumer surveys in some rural and industrial markets have shown that bundling solutions are desirable. None of the frameworks mention evaluating collective actions in sales. Collective actions have been discussed by Olson (1999) and the network perspective by Ford et al. (2002) and Gemunden et al. (1997) and may be integrated into a new framework.

Our framework for sales planning and management is presented below and some templates are given as examples for implementing it.

6.4 The Framework Proposition

The framework proposed is shown in Figure 6.1.

The sequence in Figure 6.1 organizes the major sales decisions in three different phases: sales planning and organization, manager tasks, and finally the sales control.

Step 1

This step tries to think of the strategic role of the salesperson for the firm. It starts with consumer behavior analysis and thinking of what is needed as marketing activity to satisfy the client before, during, and after the sale. The salesperson should perform some of these activities.

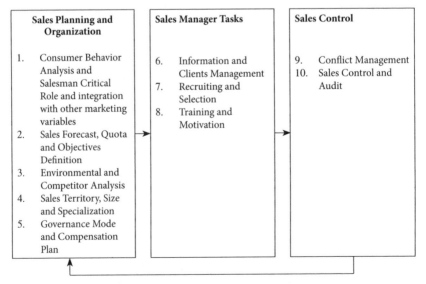

Figure 6.1 Framework for sales planning and management

Source: authors

Some firms, for instance, may stress the critical role of the salesperson providing after sales service, and instructing the client's employees, but delegating to the telemarketing center prospecting for new clients (Table 6.2).

It is important to understand what the expected roles of the salespeople are, according to the target market. Besides, when thinking about this, you need to integrate the different marketing variables in order to strengthen the marketing efforts.

Integrating sales with other marketing variables has to do with how to obtain synergy among marketing efforts. Communication activities have much to offer to salespeople for instance. Salespeople can bring new insights from the field to the creation of new messages while using advertising in their laptops for exhibition to their clients when making sales calls. Table 6.3 offers a mental method to think of marketing function integration focused on sales force activities.

Step 2

In the second phase, the sales manager may think about the objectives in terms of results and activities he or she may expect from the sales team, totally aligned with the critical role defined in Step 1.

If service providing is a critical role, then it should be represented in the salesperson's objective plan. There is no sense telling salespeople they need to provide service if this is not evident in the objective plan. Establishing objectives just for sales volumes and values is far from optimum, considering the diverse and rich possibilities of activities that the salesperson can perform.

Table 6.2 Strategic Roles of Sales Person

Buying Behavior	What Marketing Activities are Needed?	Does the Work of a Sales Man Add Value to It?	Define the Critical Role at This Point of the Sale Process
Needs identification	Ex: advertising	No	None
Information search	Ex: advertising, sales people	Yes	Sales presentation
Alternatives evaluation			
Choice			
After buying behavior			

Source: elaborated by the authors, based on Zoltners, et al. (2001) and Engel et al. (2001)

Table 6.3 Integrating Marketing and Sales Activities

Marketing Variable	What Does it Have to Offer to Sales People?	How can sales People Contribute to Improve this Marketing Variable?	Synthesis of Proposed Integration Activities
Communication	Bring new insights from the field to the creation of new messages.	Use advertising in their notebooks for exhibition to their clients when making sales calls.	Gathering Insights from sales people
Making available ads for sales calls			
Pricing			
Product			
Distribution			

Source: elaborated by the authors

Table 6.4 Sales Objective Plan

Which variables can be used?
Volume Objectives
Sales Volume ($)
Sales Physical Volume
Sales of Product Lines
Others
Activity Objectives
Visits
Letters for Prospects
Sales Proposals
Field Demonstrations
Services
Reports
Others
Financial Quotas
Sales Expenditures
Gross Margin
Net profit
Clients Net profit

Source: elaborated by the authors

Step 3

The traditional STEP (Socio-cultural, Technological, Economical and Political analysis) and competitor analysis may be done in Step 3: looking for implications for the sales force. It is important to understand how the social, technological, economic, and political aspect is impacting the efficacy of the sales method adopted by the company. The decline of an important market for the firm may force the firm to change the way it organizes the sales force, as discussed further on in the method.

Step 4

Step 4 brings the decisions to the territory level, when the type of the territory and the number of salespeople, together with the type of specialization used may be decided to each territory specifically. We may first design territories in a firm, considering the market potential. The principle is to get territories with sales potential matched up. This is needed to make the territory a control unit.

After you "split up" the territories for your firm, the next task is to estimate how many salespeople will be sent to work there. The idea is to evaluate how many visits you need to be done and how many visits an average salesperson makes per unit of time. Once you have both numbers you may divide the total number of visits by the capacity of one salesperson. To do that we have to evaluate how many clients truly deserve a sales visit and how long a sales visit will take considering the relationship policy you define for your firm.

Step 5

Step 5 brings together two very important decisions: the governance mode (the use of sales representatives or employed salespeople), and the definition of the remuneration plan (these two decisions were grouped because of the legal connection they normally have; if you have independent representatives you just pay on a variable basis). In this step Transaction Cost Economy and Agency theories may be used to make these decisions. The choice whether to use a sales representative or employed salespeople should be followed by a list of side effects related to the option made, and also, forms to minimize these side effects.

Particularly for the remuneration plan a template is given below, where some questions are mentioned. Any "yes" given for these questions means increase one of the four steps for building a remuneration plan: (1) total financial value, (2) fixed part, (3) variable part, and (4) non-financial rewards (see Figure 6.2).

Table 6.5 A Realistic Analysis on the Best Sales Governance Method

	Advantages for the Firm	*Disadvantages*
Representatives		
Employed Sales People		
	How to exploit even more the advantages	How to overcome disadvantages
Representatives		
Employed Sales People		

Source: elaborated by the authors

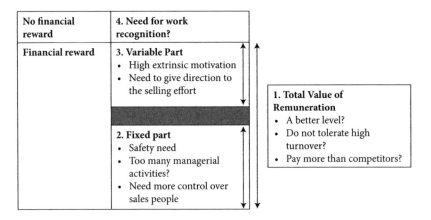

Figure 6.2 A template for remuneration plan

Source: elaborated by the authors

Continuing, the second phase highlights the sales manager's role in bridging the information between the field (clients and salesman) and the headquarters, also in acquiring and maintaining a well-prepared and motivated sales team.

Step 6

At Step 6 the firm may design the information flows from the sales force back to the firm, and in the opposite direction, the communication flow from the firm to the market. This is needed to explore the opportunities in exchanging market information and integrating the various sales levels. Many technological tools are available to speed up this process and make it as easy as possible. From the firm to the salespeople, true marketing encyclopedias are made available to enhance sales power at selling and, from the field to the firm, different forms of getting

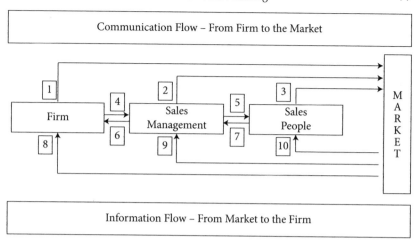

Figure 6.3 Increasing communication and information flows

Source: authors

Table 6.6 Enhancing Communication Flows

Flow	Is it a critical link?	Which tool or process can enhance communication/information flows?
1		
2		
3		
4		
5		
6		
7		
8		
9		
10		

Source: elaborated by the authors

information from salespeople (with laptops, electronic reports) allows marketing departments to adjust their sales proposals.

Also it is important that the manager implement the segment strategy of the company by selecting the most valuable clients in the territory and helping salespeople best attend to their needs to keep their loyalty. Relationship management should be implemented at this level with the help of the sales manager, showing the final consumers that the firm is there to guarantee they are getting the best possible resolution for their problems.

Steps 7 and 8

Steps 7 and 8 are related to acquire and maintain a well-prepared and motivated sales team, which may be the responsibility of regional sales managers. The sales manager should be capable of building a regional business plan modifying the firm's strategic marketing plan and communicating it to his team. This task is totally aligned with the very important leader role this person has to play at this level of sales management. The sales team has to see its manager as an ally for conquering its objectives.

The firm should prepare a good sales manager guide for instructing what is needed for this position, in the way it functions as a bridge between the firm and the sales team and the market.

Step 9

The control phase is composed of two steps. Step 9 deals with conflict management (potential multiple distribution channel conflicts, territory policies conflicts, among other very usual in daily activities in sales management). It is important the firm should anticipate which are the most common conflicts and create clear criteria for a solution. Conflicts in sales are repetitive and show where the method has allowed for a deficiency. If you do not treat it, it comes back worse and may cause trouble with important clients.

Step 10

Step 10 is when control measures are designed, and they have to be aligned with the critical salesperson role (Step 1), quota definition (Step 2), and compensation (Step 5). The control should always verify if the objectives are being met. That is why objective planning is as crucial as the remuneration plan allied to it. Otherwise the sales plan will be inconsistent.

The favorable aspects of the proposed sequence, compared to the other frameworks, could be that it stresses, at the beginning of the sequence, the governance mode to regulate the relationship between the firm and its salespeople, and tries to anticipate the side effects of this choice. Firms should think of all these steps before making decisions. Also, it offers potential interfaces among marketing variables; trying to integrate the marketing efforts in a coordinated way, when thinking of needed marketing activities for satisfying consumers. It inserts a topic of information and communication design within the sales organizational structure and inserts a topic for conflict management, dealing with channel conflict, and territorial conflicts, among others.

Summary

Sales force is a broad and well-explored field of research. However, most conceptual frameworks for sales planning and management emphasize just one aspect or another and lack managerial orientation towards an organized group of actions for sales managers. Besides, actual environmental changes ask for new considerations and a deep exploration on aspects, which are briefly discussed in general frameworks. After a short introduction on sales literature, this chapter highlights marketing changes that motivate important reflections on sales planning and management, and proposes a new framework. The proposed framework aims to organize the main tasks of the sales manager in a logical sequence of steps and consider the complexity of this particular marketing variable and its potential for creating strong relationships with most valued clients and thus gaining competitive advantage. Ten steps are presented with tables and charts to be filled in by readers.

Questions

1 Think of a salesperson of industrial products such as packaging materials and systems. How can we think of his or her strategic roles and how can we formulate an incentive system for this role? Use the proposed charts in the chapter (sections 6.2 and 6.4).
2 Give an example of marketing integration to each of the marketing variables. Use and fill in Table 6.3.
3 How does the Internet facilitate the communication and information flows needed to manage the sales team?

7

How to Strategically Build Joint Ventures

After reading this chapter, you will be able to:

- Use a six step framework to analyze and propose strategic alliances;
- Propose different business arrangements for partnerships and evaluate each of them;
- Understand critical success factors for joint ventures.

Applications:

- Joint ventures and strategic alliances formation;
- Managerial practices for joint ventures.

7.1 Introduction

Strategic alliance is a flexible way to access complementary resources and skills that reside in other companies.[1] Gulati (1998) defines strategic alliances as "voluntary arrangements between firms involving exchange, sharing, or co-development of products, technologies, or services. They can occur as a result of a wide range of motives and goals, take a variety of forms, and occur across vertical and horizontal boundaries."

Joint ventures are a special type of alliance in which a new firm is created and owned by the alliance partners. Joint ventures can help managers deal with risk in uncertain markets, share the cost of large-scale capital investments, and inject new-found entrepreneurial spirit into a maturing business.[2]

Over the last few years, thousands of joint ventures and alliances have been launched worldwide. However, there are still a lot of companies that fail in forming joint ventures. The question that often strikes managers is how to plan, implement, and overcome the many challenges inherent in forming joint ventures.

Given the complexity of joint ventures, a framework to guide the implementation can be a helpful tool. From a strategic standpoint, the implementation of joint ventures can be set up by looking at the sequence of events through the formation. This sequence includes the following seven steps: the historical analysis of the relationship, definition of market opportunities, analysis of the core competence, definition of the objective of each participant, analysis of the alternatives of coordination forms, evaluation of the critical success factors, and the design of the relationship management. The objective here is to discuss this seven-step framework to build joint ventures. We also attempt to characterize the framework for academics and practitioners to evaluate the potential for joint ventures in the future, as well as evaluate past failures and successes of joint ventures initiatives.

To accomplish this objective, a review was conducted on the literature of strategic alliances and complemented with topics about marketing channels, transactions cost economics, marketing research, and strategic management. In this chapter, to illustrate the proposed framework, a case study was developed. Two companies were followed throughout the years 2004 and 2005 in the alliance formation.

7.2 The Framework to Build Joint Ventures

The framework is illustrated below. The steps have theoretical and practical contributions, as indicated in Figure 7.1.

In the figure some theories are indicated throughout the steps. These conceptual bodies are explained in the appendix of this chapter; they provide the theoretical reasoning to organize the joint venture framework, as presented here.

From this section on, the steps will be explained in detail. An example will be given of a joint venture case between firms A and B, which had complementary products and were looking for a way to combine efforts to better explore a specific market segment.

7.2.1 History of the Relationship

The first step refers to a detailed study about the history of the past relationships between the focal company and potential candidates.

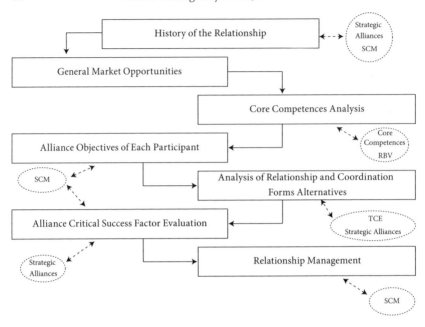

Figure 7.1 A framework to build joint ventures

Source: authors

As joint ventures are strongly dependent on the commitment and goodwill of the companies to change some of their behavior at the cost of individual benefits, the analysis of past relationships is an important step to avoid alliance failure.[3]

The evaluation of the firms' relationship is related to Gulati's (1998) point of view that a firm on its own initiative identifies the need for an alliance, identifies the best partner available, and chooses appropriate contracts to formalize the alliance. Rather, it is observed that many new opportunities for alliance were presented to firms through their existing sets of alliance partners. In the instances in which firms independently initiated new alliances, they turned to their existing relationships first for potential partners, or sought referrals from them on potential partners. Table 7.1 enumerates some points highlighting the history of companies A and B.

Companies A and B have developed an excellent relationship in the last three years. They keep a good buyer–supplier relationship and consistently share information. This is a result of more than 15 meetings, traveling, and visits, involving several persons from different areas. These meetings are important due to the fact that several alliances fail because of lack of commitment.

Table 7.1 List of Points to Discuss and Commit of the Previous Relationship

- They want to do business for a long time?
- They are willing to grow the relationship with cooperative culture?
- They will be patient with each other's mistakes?
- They have a strong sense of loyalty?
- They have similar goals, methods of operations, corporate cultures and decision-making processes?
- The higher management is committed?
- There is no threat of unfriendly takeover?
- Is it good to share financial risks of the initiative?
- They want to make long-term investments?
- They will dedicate people and efforts to the alliance?
- Rapid changes usually happen in the market?
- They will not be looking for another organization as business partner?
- If another organization appears, they will try to use their offer as a benchmark and not substitute either A or B?
- There is something very valuable to be transferred from one to another?
- A has insufficient resources to grow on its own and to reach B channels?
- Entering on its own in A market is not the best solution for B?
- Do both companies desire leadership in the market?
- The relative urgency of this relationship is the same for A and B?

Source: authors

Considering that there is already a high level of trust and commitment, the next steps will be to see and analyze the opportunities, the companies, and the governance structure.

7.2.2 General Market Opportunities

The second step is to draw on the opportunities the companies face in their business and explore how the alliance can enhance it. The market analysis should be conducted including structure maps, value added analysis, and validation of opportunities for the target market.[4] Companies A and B are discussing a strategic movement in a market.

The framework applied in the case was developed with meetings where we analyzed the market opportunities for the companies and then discussed common opportunities that could be better explored by the alliance, for example if there is a need in the market for such a company with a particular offer (product + services). Potential partners should do marketing research before advancing on the relationship.

Table 7.2 Market Needs

The market wants (under the marketing concept, what are the needs that justifies a new company or a new operation?)
• Clients need more assistance
• Final consumers and stores need a broader product line and services
• Home centers market need new products
• Urban infra-structure will grow
• The companies A and B market needs products + services offers together

Source: authors

Table 7.2 is a suggestion of market opportunities analysis, rising for the potential joint venture.

7.2.3 Core Competencies of Each Company

The definition of core competence[5] refers to the organization's learning process, especially in coordinating several production abilities and technology. The decision for diversification and entrance into a new market must be oriented by the core competence of the company. What is suggested in this step of the framework is to reflect on the core competencies of each company and place them in a table. The case of companies A and B shows some examples in Table 7.3.

The list of competencies of each company was defined after three meetings mediated by the authors. In the first meeting with directors and managers of company B alone, we discussed the competencies of company B and the opinions of the participants about company A's competencies. In the second meeting, we met solely with company A. The last meeting was a shared meeting, where the competencies of each company were listed and the participants of both companies were asked to score the competencies of their own company and the other company. The scale used was zero for a not-important competence (to the strategic alliance) to 10 for extremely important competence to the possible alliance.

After these opinions we had an open discussion about the major points where the evaluations of both future partners was very different. Why did this happen? What kind of opinions were different and how were the competencies evaluated? After this open debate, another round for point attribution was done, and opinions tended to become more equal.

Table 7.3 Consolidated Chart of Companies' Core Competencies

A	B
• Excellence in projects and innovations.	• Excellence in products.
• Intelligence in client solutions.	• Excellence in branding.
• Relationship with clients.	• Excellence in distribution (multinational coverage).
• Access to financing.	• Responsible for an input of A.
• High production scale and relative low production costs.	• High investments in P&D.

Source: authors

7.2.4 Objectives of Each Participant

For an alliance to succeed, three initial conditions are necessary. First, and most important, is that there must be a need in the market. Under the marketing concept, initiatives should be built if there is a need for them. The second and third are related to particular wishes of the companies involved.

In order to be successful, firms in an alliance must mutually agree on processes and objectives before starting an alliance project. An emphasis would be on the normal inter-firm knowledge transfer that happens.[6] Table 7.4 shows needs of the case presented in this chapter, evaluating the objectives of companies A and B.

The definition of objectives followed a process similar to the competencies definition. Each company must set their objectives separately. The difference here is that the companies stated their own objectives and also speculated on the objectives of the other company for the alliance.

It is an interactive process that makes companies think about the purposes of a partner when entering into a partnership. After these definitions, an open debate was done again, so that the objectives of each company could be openly discussed and comprehended.

We suggest keeping these procedures and evaluating if the three conditions listed above are applicable. The next step attempts to study the possible arrangements for the joint initiative between B and A.

Table 7.4 Who Needs What from the Alliance?

A wants:	B wants:
• To grow faster in the market.	• To grow in the "company A" market using strategic alliance (complementarities with other company).
• To improve market coverage.	• To add value to its sales.
• To operate in new business.	• New products.
• To be present in public projects.	• New business.
• More penetration in retail.	• New technologies.
• To launch new products.	• To offer complete solutions.
	• To attend different needs of different market segments.
	• More access to governmental financing projects.

Source: authors

7.2.5 Analysis of Relationship and Coordination Forms Alternatives

While alliances may be considered a distinct form of governance that is different from markets or hierarchies, there is also considerable variation in the formal structure of alliances themselves.[7]

This step is to confront the joint venture option with other possible arrangements. In this case, two alternatives will be raised. The first one is a joint venture, which is a kind of strategic alliance where two original companies (A and B) build a third one, C, and the two originals continue to exist (if they did not, it would be a merger). The second alternative is having B invest in A's capital, in an amount up to 49%.

Table 7.5 presents a synthesis of the possible advantages of the joint venture. The same analysis could be done for the merger option, and they would have to be faced. As it is a summary, we will show just the reflections on the joint venture option to serve as an example. In general, this solution is quicker to form and develop, less risky, more flexible to operate and enables stretching financial, managerial, and technical resources. It is a way to increase sales without too many investments and without a large increase in overhead costs.

Table 7.5 Joint Venture Possible Advantages to Companies

B	A
• Would be able to grow in its market segment using the strategic alliance, adding value to its current product line	• Would outsource marketing (communication, sales, distribution and staff) costs to C
• Acquire technology from A	• Grow faster in the market
• Increase speed of operations	• Double resources and investments
• Risk sharing	• Double management capacity
• Outsource marketing costs designated to the market segment to C	• More penetration in retail using channels of B
• Since it would be more linked to final clients, it will be able to launch new products and services with more efficiency.	• To launch new products to new market segments using B channels
• Together with A, offer complete solutions, trying to produce other components that today are supplied by other companies	• The focus on family and small farmers market with adapted products using B channels could be improved.
• To attend different needs of different market Segments	
• To attend complementarities with other company	
• To be linked to a strong partner since there is high lead time to develop A products	
• More access to governmental financing projects	

Source: authors

7.2.6 Alliance Critical Success Factors Evaluation and Relationship Management

This step identifies factors within the firm's market environment that determine its ability to survive and prosper (its key success factors) and to develop guidelines for the relationship management for the companies and the joint venture.[8]

These analyses and management decisions are very important because such management decisions may influence the future and the performance of the alliance. Gulati (1998) argues that the performance of alliances has received less attention than others areas. While issues concerning the management of individual alliances are still important and merit further consideration, new issues resulting from managing the portfolio of alliance have arisen. Table 7.6 shows the critical success

Table 7.6 Critical Success Factors—Conditions to Succeed for Company C (Getting Over Disadvantages)

- Architecture of the joint venture must be very well done
- Critical driving forces (human resources, marketing, finance) should be addressed and agreed by A and B
- Strategic questions like mission, strengths and weaknesses, and trends must be jointly discussed and agreed
- Organizational culture should be addressed, in factors related to time orientation, technology, communications, information flow, organizational structure, labor and style of A and B
- Risks of problems in relationship between A and B should be considered
- Risks of acquisition should be considered
- Operational integration should be done
- Double taxing should be equalized (disadvantage)
- Discuss market risks, in case of lower expectations for B or A
- Discuss A and B risks of changing management and the new management not being interested in continuing the joint venture
- Discuss competitive technology risks (in the company C segment), since this will be one of the businesses of B, and the only business of A
- Control methods should be very well discussed and agreed by A and B
- Management skills must be aggressive and marketing oriented to reach advantages listed
- Resources should be committed and capital risks should be addressed
- Risk of technology (production + projects) transfer from A to B should be considered.
- Risk of marketing channels transfer from B to A should be considered
- B is involved in all other segments that compete with C. There is a risk in the future of more investments of B in other segments that would be prejudicial to C.
- Build up a leadership strategy, being pioneers, making things happen, entailing spirit and enthusiasm, risk taking and others
- Both brands should be maintained in the joint venture due to their power and awareness
- Consider if B products would be only available to C and not to competitors of C (or at least price policies for competitors)
- Risks of C competitors (clients of B today)
- Price of A and B products to C should have a policy and be very well discussed (transfer prices policies)
- Risks of channels conflicts, that will happen, must be considered. B and A may have different relationships with channels. How will it be with C?
- Who will develop new products demanded by C? B or A? This question should be discussed

Source: authors

factors for the joint venture. Both companies should discuss each of these.

This poses questions about what such capabilities are and what systematic tactics firms might use to internalize such capabilities. At least some of these capabilities include (as regarded in this framework): identifying valuable alliances opportunities and good partners, using appropriate governance mechanisms, developing inter-firm knowledge sharing routines, making requisite relationship-specific asset investments, and initiating necessary changes to the partnership as it evolves while also managing partner expectations.

Bamford, Ernst & Fubini (2004) regard the process of building and managing the organization (a cohesive, high performing joint venture or alliance) as a great challenge, when most managers come from, will want to return to, and may even hold simultaneous positions in the parent companies. Many venture CEOs lament that alliances are treated as dumping grounds for under-performing executives, rather than as magnets for high-potential managers. Most companies that complete a merger dedicate a full-time team of their best leaders to integrate the target company. By contrast, the launch teams of many joint ventures comprise a handful of part-time managers who are learning as they go.

Some guidelines for launching, launch planning and execution apply to all joint ventures and alliances. The parent companies should appoint a launch leader and identify deal champions. The latter are typically senior executives from each parent company who are known and respected across the organization and who have a strong interest in the success of the joint venture. The parent companies should also assemble a dedicated and experienced transition team immediately upon signing the memorandum of understanding. This team is responsible for getting the business up and running. Its tasks include developing a detailed business plan, creating a roadmap that orchestrates the activities of all work groups, and intervening when the launch process veers off track.

Summary

There is an overall concern about how alliances are formed. In this chapter, we discussed a framework to guide firms in their process of joint venture formation. In the search for competitive advantages, companies form joint ventures to better explore the competencies and to join efforts expanding their businesses and exploiting synergies. The framework presented in this chapter contains seven steps and was completely applied in a formation of a joint venture between two companies, whose identity was preserved. This sequence includes the following steps: the historical analysis of the relationship, definition of market opportunities, analysis of the core competence, definition of the objective of each participant, analysis of the alternatives of coordination forms, evaluation of the critical success factor, and the design of the relationship management. Managers may use this framework to guide their decision-making process along the joint venture formation. There are high costs in the phase of elaborating a contract, defining objectives and setting the necessary safeguards. Once managers are able to systematically make their decisions, the chances of success are rather high.

Questions

1   Think of a possible strategic alliance between your company and a potential partner and apply the seven-step framework for joint venture creation.

2   Choose an example of a known successful strategic alliance in your market. Using the seven-step framework tips, why do you think it was successful?

3   Using Table 7.6 (Critical success factors of joint ventures) give an example of failure based on the topics commented on in the table.

8

A Method for Building Competitive Advantage via Marketing Channels Incentives

After reading this chapter, you will be able to:

- Build an incentive system to align strategies of your distributors with your firm;
- Understand the rationale behind incentive systems used in marketing channels;
- Take a strategic and long-term view of how to improve the marketing channel performance, increasing their commitment with the supplier firm.

Applications:

- Marketing channels planning;
- Marketing channel management.

8.1 Introduction

Why is it important to develop cooperation with distributors? A distributor is the one who takes the product to the final consumer, making it available and in a good condition. It is a fundamental part of the marketing effort. A well-coordinated group of distributors may indicate an important source of competitive advantage based on services, in a scenario where products are more and more equal.

The distribution variable in the marketing mix, when badly designed, does not allow the firm to succeed in its objectives related to consumer satisfaction and retention. Out of necessity, firms use distributors. However, it is always important to remember that a distributor is a different firm, which most commonly has different vision, values, and skills. Thus, to enable cooperation between two interdependent firms (supplier and distributor) you need the creation of the right set of incentives. This chapter explores ways to create cooperation and how a supplier must work towards it.

In the following theoretical introduction, first marketing channels and their functions are conceptualized. Second, a reflection is made regarding the existence of indirect marketing channels, and third, a characterization of the relationship between supplier and distributor is made in order to understand the motivations behind it, for both sides. Finally, we show the relationship and network perspective together with marketing incentives.

8.2 Marketing Incentives and Objectives Alignment with Distributors

Marketing incentive is a way to stimulate higher productivity of the sales or distributor team through prize offerings. It may be applied to several roles, such as salespeople, employees, distributors, and distributors' salespeople.[1]

Simply, an incentive program may be looked at as rewards for something done, typically prizes for sales volume. The down side of it is that it may create an "addiction" to the incentive program, and not create the expected effect of cooperation between a supplier and a distributor. For this reason, the vision must be wider. The American Marketing Association (AMA) defines marketing incentives as: "An event offering rewards or inducements to stimulate the salesforce or channel members to achieve predetermined sales, profit, distribution, or other goals." By this definition, it may be possible to work with incentives to induce or stimulate the distributors to work into the direction desired by the supplier.

Marketing incentives programs may be used to enhance the global performance of the marketing channel, not just the financial result. For the distributor performance evaluation, the templates related to marketing flows, seen in Figure 4.1, can be used.

The central objective topic of this chapter is to propose a sequence of steps for designing incentives for marketing channels.

The chapter relates marketing channels with marketing incentives. It explores the marketing relationship theory oriented to relationship marketing and networks.

8.3 Proposition of a Method for Designing Incentives for Distributors

This topic intends to suggest a method of analysis, which should be done to develop the right set of incentives for distributors. As discussed in the introduction of this chapter, the literature is rich with ways of creating incentives for sales forces. In this chapter, this literature is applied to marketing channels. The contribution of it is developing a strategy to align the objectives of marketing channels and their suppliers and improve the chain performance.

We propose a sequence of five steps (Figure 8.1). First, it is important to define the objectives of the supplier with the channel member. Second, a diagnostic of the actual situation of the channel members might be done, assuming a supplier perspective. Third, the performance measures should be created, and in the fourth step, the benefits related to the achievement of the performance measures should be created. In the final step, the supplier should communicate the incentive program and implement and control it.

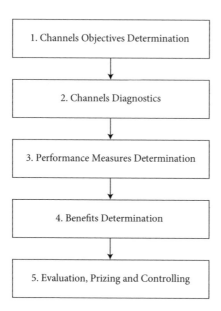

Figure 8.1 A sequence for designing incentives for distributors

Source: authors

8.3.1 Defining Objectives with Channel Members

An analysis should be done related to what is expected from the channel member, in the relationship with his supplier, at performing activities such as product and services delivery, communication efforts, information gathering, sales results, funding final consumers, among others.

For this analysis a more detailed list of each marketing flow is important because it functions as a checklist for the supplier: if the listed activity should or should not, or could or could not be performed by the distributor. If this is so, a second decision is if this particular activity deserves a specific incentive. The detailed list of marketing flows along with the reasoning for building the incentive program is shown in Table 8.1 (pages 96–97).

8.3.2 Diagnostic of Actual Channel Member Performance at a Supplier Perspective

Once the supplier has a clear understanding of what is expected from the distributor, it is important to understand the current channel member performance and to compare it to the desired channel member performance.

A high channel member motivation to go from the current to the desired performance level is exactly the role the incentive program should play.

8.3.3 Designing Performance Measures

Between an ideal situation and a desired one, there will be a set of improvements developed by the distributor. What is an unsatisfactory, reasonable, good, or excellent performance should be known by the supplier. The supplier should clearly signal to the distributor the performance requisites and their levels of achievement and consequently the reward for it.

Certainly, the more quantitative and observable a performance measure is, the lower the subjective judgment presented in the incentive programs. However, some activities (such as contribution to marketing information gathering) are difficult to make operational in a quantitative measure. Others, like sales volume or margin, are easily evaluated quantitatively.

The definition of a performance measure might suppose some distributors are weak on those criteria, others are reasonable, and still others are very strong. The question is what is a weak, reasonable, or strong performance in a certain criteria? How can the supplier transform this performance expectation in measures easily communicated to the distributor?

In Table 8.1, some marketing flows are shown in a more detailed way. After that, for each activity there are questions for those who are creating the incentive program, following the proposed steps. What is the expected performance, and consequently the objective, in such an activity? What is the current situation? What are the requisites or measures for that activity?

8.3.4 Benefits Design

Once the performance measures are defined and a first evaluation is done, the level of benefits according to the level of success achievement must be clearly defined. When the supplier states the benefits for the distributor, the supplier is motivating the distributor to improve exactly on the aspects related to the improvement of the supplier–distributor relationship.

To have a strong effect the benefits offered by the supplier have to be of a true value for the distributor. It is important to take a look at the relationship marketing theory applied for the industrial segment.

The benefits generated might be related to the financial advantages (discounts, better payment conditions, bonus in products), structural advantages (consulting, sales training, promotional material, joint promotion activities) and social (social events, parties, trips, clubs) as proposed by Berry (1983). The supplier may elaborate a package of benefits according to the classification of the distributor, for example: excellent performers get the best package of "gold benefits," good performers, get a package of "silver benefits," and so on, as seen in Table 8.2.

The most important thing is the clear understanding by the distributor of the path to be followed to become a gold distributor and receive the gold package of benefits. If that happens, the group of distributors will work to improve their services and activities into the direction desired by the supplier. This incentive alignment effect is shown in Table 8.3.

Table 8.1 Objectives, Actual Situation and Performance Measures for Activities related to Marketing Flows in Marketing Channels

Function	What is the Objective?	What is the Actual Situation?	Which are the Performance Measures?
Product and Services Flow Variables			
Management and inventory levels (An Example)	A high level of inventory for the supplier products.	Very heterogeneous. Missing important lines.	Certain number of tons for each product line every month is excellent, 10% less than this is good, 20% reasonable, 30% is bad, 40% is terrible.
Product transportation			
Product modification			
Product line and variety			
Evaluation of new products			
Predicted volume of sales (performance)			
Technical support of explanation/installation			
After-sales service			
Providing of sales (team) service			
Training: scope and costs			
Maintenance and product repair			
Packaging subjects/specifications			
Brand subjects			
Exclusivity details found in the contract			
Territorial rights found in the contract			
Predictable market coverage			
Duration (period to perform the flows)			
Adaptation to specific laws			
Others (fill in)			
Communications Flow Variables			
Advertisement (all forms)			

Sales promotion (all)

Public relations actions (all)

Direct marketing actions

Providing information about products

Sharing in communications budget

Communication within direct sales

Packaging information

Others (fill in)

Information Flow Variables

Providing information about consumer's market

Providing information about competitors

Providing information about changes in the environment

Participation in the planning process

Frequency and quality in information

Providing complaints information

Electronic orders

Others (fill in)

Payments and Orders Flows

Order frequency

Pricing policies and payments

Margins analysis

Commissions (volume and frequency)

Conducting credits to final consumers

Billing customers

Search for financing sources

Pricing guarantees

Others (fill in)

Source: adapted from Neves (2003)

Table 8.2 Marketing Channel Benefit Packages

Performance Level	Benefits
A	**Package A** Financial Benefits (price discount, credit) Services Support in Communication Product Bonification
B	**Package B** Financial Benefits (price discount, credit) Services Support in Communication Product Bonification
C	**Package C** Financial Benefits (price discount, credit) Services Support in Communication Product Bonification

Source: elaborated by the authors

Table 8.3 Creation of a Virtuous Cycle

Performance Level	Benefits
Dealer A	What should I keep doing for not losing the level of benefits I have?
Dealer B	What should I do to obtain Package A of benefits? Following the target channel performance!
Dealer C	What should I do to obtain Package B of incentives? Following the target channel performance

Source: elaborated by the authors

8.3.5 Implementation, Prizes, and Control

Once the performance measures are created, the program must be implemented. According to the classification of the distributor, it may receive a package of benefits (as discussed above).

It is important to highlight the instruction role that this incentive program may have. Imagine the distributor has been classified at a lower level of performance, and consequently receives a lower benefit. It is up to the supplier to orient and coordinate the distributor to improve and obtain a better package of benefits at the next evaluation. This is how improvement starts, and the definition of a good partnership between the supplier and distributor continues. If the incentive program is well formulated the distributor also understands that the improvement on the performance measures is also important to the improvement of the whole firm, in addition to receiving benefits from the supplier. The supplier has in its sales team a fundamental role to implement and manage it as discussed by Hutt & Speh (2002) and Levitt (1983).

8.4 Conclusions

As shown in this chapter, it is possible to create a theory related to marketing channels and incentives to understand how to develop relationships with distributors and to invent an incentive program to improve all channel members' performances. The existent dimensions and functions of the theoretical line of marketing channels creates the understanding of relationships between supplier, distributor, and the marketing flow. Marketing incentives show how incentives may be used to influence expected behavior through extrinsic motivation. We have also discussed how relationship marketing brings ways to create strong and durable ties with valuable clients.

Building cooperation among organizations is a process that might be initiated by one side and the other must have goodwill towards it. This chapter offered a method from the supplier side to create a logical and rational mechanism to influence the distributors' behavior and to make their objectives align with the supplier's objectives.

The majority of channel conflicts between suppliers and distributors, apart from natural disputes for price bargaining, are related to the different perspectives and different objectives between both parties. This method may work as a way to learn how to improve the relationship.

It is worth noting that the supplier–distributor relationship is a result relationship. There are important legal limits for determining performance measures in a commercial relationship. It is important to submit the incentive program to a proper legal review before implementing it.

Summary

This chapter highlights the importance of creating the right set of marketing incentives as a way to foster the relationship with distributors, and consequently offer final clients the highest possible value. To understand how marketing incentives may be used, you should first conceptualize marketing channels and understand the nature of supplier–distributor relationships, to bring together different ways suppliers have to achieve good performance.

Questions

1   How is an incentive program different for sales teams and for distributors?
2   Choose a particular industry where channel members are important at delivering product and services to the final consumer. Describe in general terms the content of an incentive program to be used by a supplier with his channel members.
3   What should you do if a channel member is always valued in the worst category? Think of additional rules for increasing incentives.

9

Identifying Key Success Factors to Develop Market-Driven Strategies

After reading this chapter, you will be able to:

- Understand the prerequisites for success in a market-driven firm;
- Apply a tool[1] to evaluate consumer needs and compare your company with competitors on the capacity to answer these needs;
- Make an internal marketing audit based on consumer needs and key success factors.

Applications:

- Marketing internal audit;
- Competitor analysis;
- Demand analysis;
- Strategy.

9.1 Introduction

The key success factor (KSF) is a tool used to understand customers' needs and at the same time reflect on the resources and competencies necessary to satisfy these needs. For the simple reason that a firm is almost never alone in the market, how the main competitors regard these resources and competencies in relation to the focal company is of fundamental importance. The tool allows people to think strategically about clients and competitors and helps the firm to focus on what really matters in the market.

The key success factors framework (e.g. the Porter Five Forces framework) is usually used to complete the analysis of an industry's profit potential. It is used because managers need to understand how the industry profit is shared among different firms competing in that industry. The success of a particular firm will lead to increasing sales and repeated purchases by its clients and therefore it will increase profit share.

Grant (2001) presents a discussion of industry dynamics and competition between industry participants, which is ultimately a battle for competitive advantage in which firms rival one another to attract customers and maneuver for positional advantage. Managers need to identify those factors within the firm's market environment that determine its ability to survive and prosper. We will call them "key success factors."

To survive and prosper in an industry, a firm must meet two criteria: first, it must supply what customers want to buy, and second, it must survive the competition. Hence, we may start by asking two questions (Grant, 2001) (see Figure 9.1):

What do our customers want?

What does the firm need to do to survive competition?

To answer the first question we need to look more closely at customers of the industry and view them not so much as a source of bargaining power—and hence as a threat to profitability—but more as the basic raison d'être of the industry and as the underlying source of profit.

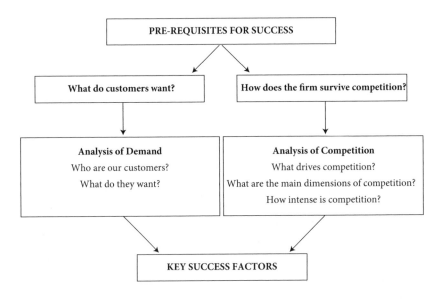

Figure 9.1 Identifying key success factors

Source: Grant (2001)

This implies that the firm must identify who the customers are, determine their needs, and establish the basis on which they select the offerings of one supplier over those of another.

Once we have identified the basis of customers' preference, this is merely the starting point for a chain of analysis. For example, if consumers' choice of supermarkets is based primarily on which offer lowest prices, and if the ability to offer low prices depends on low costs, the key issues concern the determinants of costs among supermarkets.

Therefore, in order to start identifying the key success factors, we suggest that managers and analysts complete a list of customers' wants as related to the market in which they compete.

Since companies are playing in different market segments, separated analysis must be done for each segment. Table 9.1 can help detail this list.

The second question requires that the firm examines the basis of competition in the industry. How intense is competition and what are its key dimensions? Thus, in the luxury car market, consumers select primarily on the basis of prestige, design, quality, and exclusivity. However, these qualities are an insufficient basis for success. In this intensely competitive market, survival requires a strong financial position (to finance new product development) and costs that are sufficiently low to allow a company to cover its cost of capital.

According to Grant (2001), key success factors can also be identified through the direct modeling of profitability. In the same way that Porter's five forces analysis determines industry-level profitability, we can also attempt to model firm-level profitability in terms of identifying the key factors that drive a firm's relative profitability within an industry.

Some progress can be made on this front, by disaggregating a firm's return on capital in use into individual operating factors and ratios; we can pinpoint the most important determinants of a firm's success. In many industries, these primary drivers of firm-level profitability are well known and widely used as performance targets.

Table 9.1 Customer Wants Analysis

*Market Segment:*_____
1
2
...
n

Source: authors

Table 9.2 Company Resource and Capabilities to Overcome Competitors

Market Segment:_____
1
2
...
n

Source: authors

The objective here in identifying key success factors is less ambitious. There is no universal blueprint for a successful strategy, and even in individual industries, there is no "generic strategy" that can guarantee superior profitability. However, each market is different in terms of what motivates customers and how competition works. Understanding these aspects of the industry environment is a prerequisite for an effective business strategy.

Nevertheless, this does not imply that firms within an industry adopt common strategies. Since every firm comprises a unique set of resources and capabilities, even when an industry is subject to common success factors (e.g. low costs), firms will select unique strategies to link their resources and capabilities to industry success factors. To assist your analysis, fill in Table 9.2.

Together, the analysis of Tables 9.1 and 9.2 can help managers understand and identify key factors. In this way a key success factor is something that consolidates what customers want and how a company uses its resources and capabilities to perform in the market.

For example, in a certain market segment, customers want to buy products at low prices and the company is developing programs to reduce production/distribution costs. In this case, key success factors could be access to, and good relationships with, suppliers, production scale and production process capabilities. We suggest that your analysis considers a number of key success factors, usually ranging from 4 to 10.

It is important to understand that the exercise of thinking first "what consumers want" and then "what the firm may do to overcome its competitor" might be sequential and related. We mean that if consumers want customized services, most probably the available services, quality of personnel, and good services procedures are the resources and capabilities related to these specific needs. The same reasoning should be done for a second need, let us say payment conditions, which in turn might be related to financial capacity and so on. At the end, we have a list of fundamental resources and capabilities that once consolidated might originate the key success factor. Table 9.3 illustrates this reasoning.

Additional analysis can be done, comparing the performance of the company with some competitors in the same key success factors. It gives an overview about the competitive position of the company. Table 9.4 exemplifies a framework that can be used in this analysis.

The framework to analyze the key success factors involves defining a weight for each factor. The assumption here is that even though all KSFs are important, there are factors that contribute more to the company's success.

The next step is giving a score for each factor for the company and for the main competitors. The score varies between 1 (low performance in the factor) to 10 (very good performance in the factor). After that, it

Table 9.3 Relating Consumer Needs, Competitor Analysis and Key Success Factors

What Do Consumes Want?	What Does the Firm Do to Overcome Competitors?	Key Success Factors? (Shall We Consolidate the List of Factors?)
Customized services	Available services, quality of personnel and good services procedures	Available services
Quality of personnel		
Good services procedures		
Payment conditions	Financial capacity	Financial capacity
A competitive price low price	Cost structure	Cost structure

Source: elaborated by the authors

Table 9.4 Comparing Company and Competitors—Key Success Factors (KSF)

		Company		Competitor #1		...	Competitor # n	
Key Success Factors	Weight	Score	WxS	Score	WxS	...	Score	WxS
KSF #1								
KSF #2								
KSF #3								
...								
...								
KSF #n								
Total	**100**	-	Σ	-	Σ	-	-	Σ

Source: authors

is possible to evaluate the total score of each company, calculating the score times the weight for each key success factor.

It is important that the result of the analysis indicates where exactly the firm must excel to compete properly in the market. Figure 9.2 gives an example of how to demonstrate this inside the firm to adjust strategies. In the graph, the result for each KSF is compared to the evaluation of the main competitor. If you are firm B in the example it is obvious the need to improve is mainly on technical salespeople, credit for clients, and product mix. The other factors are equal to firm A.

After this exercise it is important that the firm is able to produce an action list regarding possible marketing strategies to overcome weaknesses and explore strengths (Table 9.5), redefining marketing strategies.

We may also use two important tools suggested by Porter (1990) (Five Forces Model) and expanded by Gray at al. (2004) (Value Chain) to link intended strategy and needed activities and capabilities to excel in a

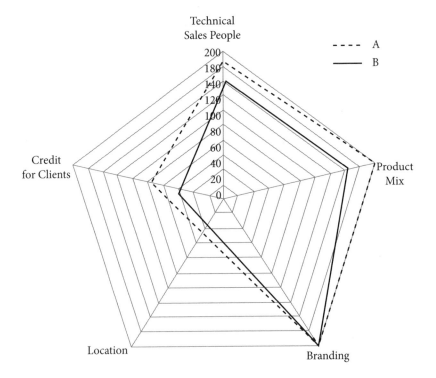

Figure 9.2 Example of key success factors for internal analysis based on competitors' reference

Source: elaborated by the authors

Table 9.5 Weakness and Strengths Related to Key Success Factors

Weaknesses on Key Success Factors	Strengths on Key Success Factors	Potential Marketing Strategies (How Do we Have to Change?)

Source: elaborated by the authors

certain market. Expanding the model understood so far, what we are suggesting is that once we understand consumer needs and competitors, we may opt for a basic strategy since we believe we are potentially better off, considering our objectives, clients, and competitors. The two following Tables (9.6 and 9.7) give us a good understanding regarding the relationship between chosen strategy and the fundamental orientation of activities and competencies within the firm. These two Tables may help find this important connection. Therefore, if a firm finds low price as a fundamental need of the customer, it may impact activities all over the firm as well as managers' capabilities. We need to think carefully what the fundamental key success factors are.

Summary

This chapter proposed an important tool called Key Success Factor. It drives the firm's attention to where investment should be made. Instead of just thinking about which attributes are used by consumers to decide among firms, it goes a step further by proposing where the firm should invest to excel in those important attributes. The analysis starts by questioning consumers about the most important criteria (what do consumers want?) and then questioning the firm on how to operate to be better than the competition at these specific criteria (how to overcome competitors at particular criteria). This means a focus on the real causes of success and not on the consequences.

Questions

1   Choose a particular firm and fill in Table 9.3, relating the analysis of customer needs and competitor analysis.

Table 9.6 Understanding the Link Between Strategy and the Fundamental Orientation of Activities Within the Firm

	Support Activities				Primary Activities				
	Infrastructure	Human Resources	Technology	Procurement	Inbound Logistics	Operations	Outbound Logistics	MKT	Services
Cost	Cost-effective management information systems (MIS). Few managerial layers. Simplified planning practices.	Consistent policies to reduce turnover. Intense focus on training employees to be efficient and multi-skilled.	Easy-to-use production technologies. Investment in technology that improves production efficiencies.	Procedures to find the lowest cost inputs. Frequent evaluation of suppliers' performances.	Efficient systems to link supplier products with production processes.	Use of economies of scale. Construction of efficient scale facilities.	Delivery schedule that reduces costs. Selection of low-cost carriers.	Small, highly trained sales force. Products priced to generate sales volume.	Efficient quality control to reduce buyer complaints.
Innovation	Highly developed MIS to capture customer preferences. Firm-wide focus on high-quality products.	Compensation encourages creativity. Subjective performance measures. Superior training.	Strong capability in basic research. Investment in technologies that allow for production of highly differentiated products.	Procedures to find the highest quality inputs. Purchase of highest quality replacement parts. Strict standards for suppliers.	Superior handling to minimize damage and improve quality.	Consistent production of attractive products. Rapid response to customers' production demands.	Accurate and responsive order processing. Rapid and timely deliveries.	Extensive granting of credit buying. Extensive personal relationships with buyers.	Extensive buyer training to assure max. value from product.
Intimacy	Highly developed MIS to capture customer preferences. Firm-wide focus on high-quality products.	Compensation encourages creativity. Subjective performance measures. Superior training.	Strong capability in basic research. investment in Technologies that allow for production of highly differentiated products.	Procedures to find the highest quality inputs. Purchase of highest quality replacement parts. Strict standards for suppliers.	HUMAN RESOURCES Field marketing training. Extensive sales support	FIRM INFRA-STRUCTURE Customer relationship management systems/support. Supply chain software	Guaranteed delivery schedules. Source documentation / verification	Customer specific value bundles. Team sales support	Joint customer-centric R&D. Automatic returns/replacement

Source: Gray, Boehlje and Akridge (2004)

Table 9.7 Linking Strategy with Fundamental Competences Within the Firm Using the 5 Forces Model

	Actual Competitors	Suppliers Bargaining Power	Buyers Power	Substitutes products	New Entrants
Cost	Managers must be able to operate with low prices better than their rival competitors.	They need to be able to absorb or not be subjected to price pressures and bargaining power of suppliers.	They should be able to sustain or mitigate the price pressure that results from buyer power better than their competitors.	They must use various techniques to deepen customer relationships and thwart customers switching to substitute products or suppliers.	They must be able to thwart or offset the threat of new entrants by barriers including continuous improvement in efficiency to lower cost;
Innovation	Mitigate rivalry by developing customer loyalty that reduces price sensitivity.	Mitigate supplier power by having the capacity to pass on input price increases or have adequate volume to negotiate lower input prices.	Reduce the power of buyers by providing a unique product or service so that buyers do not have good alternatives.	Reduce the potential of substitutes through continuous innovation and improvement in both product and process.	Mitigate the threat of new entrants by being a dominant player in the market with loyal customers and superior product and service.
Intimacy	Mitigate rivalry by developing and constantly deepening unique relationships with individual customers.	Mitigate supplier power through joint ventures and strategy alliances, and by becoming one of their key accounts or key customers.	Reduce the power of buyers by involving them in joint R&D and other activities to increase their switching costs.	Reduce the potential of substitutes by constantly searching for and introducing new products and services tailored specifically to the targeted customers.	Reduce the threat of new entrants by focusing on and dominating niches that are not large enough to attract competitors

Source: Gray, Boehlje and Akridge (2004)

2 What are the potential problems of implementing the Key Success Factors using a firm's internal people to fill in the tables and judge from performance?

3 Do you believe in fundamental changes in consumer needs or competitor analysis when a different segment is targeted in the company? How can this tool be useful to help the firm decide whether or not to target a certain market segment?

Notes

1 How to Describe the Company as an Integrated Network

1 Here we assume the supply chain as being the group of suppliers and suppliers of suppliers. There are several authors who use this term referring to the total network or value chain. We prefer to differentiate what is supply from what is marketing for reasons we expect to make clear at the end of this chapter.

3 How to Build Competitive Advantage through a Marketing Channel Plan

1 The studied sequences were Stern et al. (1996), Rosenbloom (1999), Berman (1996), and Kotler (1997).
2 Supply chain contributions came from Gattorna & Walters (1996), Ziggers, Trienekens & Zuurbier (1998), and Trienekens & Zuurbier (1996), among others.
3 Bello & Lohtia (1995), Klein et al. (1990), Kozak & Cohen (1997), and interviews.
4 Some useful insights can be given by Kumar et al. (1992), Spriggs (1994), Berman (1996), Stern et al. (1996), Rosenbloom (1999), and Gattorna & Walters (1996).

4 How to Analyze Channel Value Capture

1 The following methods, evaluation, and planning systems were studied: Method of channel decisions—Lewis (1968); Method (Theory) of Channel Control—Bucklin (1973); Structure of Adjusting Channel Strategies in Industrial Markets—Hahn & Chang (1992); Analysis of the Structure-Output Paradigm—Bucklin, Ramaswamy & Majumdar (1996); Method for Distribution Channel Planning—Neves (1999); Method of Value Appropriation Analysis by Channel Members—Souza (2002); Method of Channel Efficiency—Coughlan et al. (2002).

5 How to Build and Review Marketing and Network Contracts

1 Simon (1961) in Williamson (1985).

2 The asset specificity analysis is also present in the marketing channel plan discussed in Chapter 3. Here we go into a more detailed level, aiming solely at improving marketing contracts and not a whole and complete marketing channel plan.
3 A further analysis on power is found in El-Ansary & Stern (1972), Lusch (1976), Hunt & Nevin (1974).

6 How to Build Competitive Advantage through Sales Force Planning

1 Dubinsky (1980), Dwyer et al. (2000), Weitz et al. (2004), Kotler (2000), Etzel (2001), Churchill et al. (2000), Futrell (2003), Ingram et al. (2002), Honeycutt (2002), Zeyl (2002), Dawes (2001), Cravens (1995), Engels et al. (2000), Sheth et al. (2001), and Robinson et al. (1967).
2 Rangaswamy et al. (1990), Shapiro (1995), Zoltners et al. (2001), Lodish (1971), Albers (2000), Skiera & Albers (2000), Sinha & Zoltners (2001) Olson et al. (2001), Ingram & LaForge (1992), Dalrymple & Cron (1992), Georges (2002), Winer (1973), Anderson & Weitz (1986), Anderson (1985), Coughlan (2001), Besanko (2000), and Ryans & Weinberg (1981).
3 Morgan (2001), Jones et al. (2002), Atkinsons & Higgins (1988), Ingram & Bellenger (1982), and Chonko et al. (1992).

7 How to Strategically Build Joint Ventures

1 Definition given by Dyer, Kale & Singh (2001).
2 These concepts are found in Kemp (1999) and Bamford, Ernst & Fubini (2004).
3 This discussion is found in Coughlan et al. (2001) and Ring & van de Ven (1994).
4 These suggestions came from Corbett, Blackburn & Wassenhove (1999).
5 For a complete discussion on core competencies see Prahalad & Hamel (1990).
6 Corbett, Blackburn & Wassenhove (1999) and Mowery et al. (1996).
7 For a complete discussion on this topic, see Powell (1990).
8 See Grant (2002) for a complete discussion on inter-organizational relationship management. Also, Spekman et al. (1998) give important contributions of an adequate relationship configuration and implementation. Also the research done by Inkpen & Beamish (1997) developed an interesting framework to evaluate instability of international joint ventures, based on power and dependence. The authors conclude that instability increases with imbalance.

8 A Method for Building Competitive Advantage via Marketing Channels Incentives

1 For a full discussion on Marketing Incentives see Crescitelli (2002).

9 Identifying Key Success Factors to Develop Market-Driven Strategies

1 Framework developed by authors based on Grant (2001). This framework was applied in more than 50 companies, including BASF, Netafim Brasil, and Fri-Ribe.

References and Further Reading

Aaker, D. A. & Day, G. S. *Marketing Research*. Chichester: John Wiley and Sons, 3rd edition, 1982.

Achrol, R. S. & Stern, L. W. Environmental Determinants of Decision Making Uncertainty in Marketing Channels. *Journal of Marketing Research*, v. 25, p. 36–50, 1988.

Albers, S. Sales-Force Management. In: Blois, K. (Ed.): *The Oxford Textbook of Marketing*. Oxford: Oxford University Press, p. 292–317, 2000a.

Albers, S. The Choice Between Employed Salespersons and Independent Manufacturer Representatives. In: Albach, H. et al. (Eds): *Theory of the Firm*. Springer: Berlin, p. 169–184, 2000b.

Alderson, W. Factors Governing the Development of Marketing Channels. In: Clewett, R. M. *Marketing Channels in Manufactured Products*. Homewood: Richard D. Irwin, p. 5–22, 1954..

AMA. American Marketing Association. Available at www.marketingpower.com. Accessed 22 September 2004.

Anderson, E. The Salesperson as Outside Agent or Employee: A Transaction Cost Analysis. *Marketing Science*, v. 4, p. 234–253, 1985.

Anderson, E. Strategic Implications of Darwinian Economics for Selling Efficiency and Choice of Integrated or Independent Sales Forces. *Management Science*, v. 34, n. 5, p. 599–618, May 1988.

Anderson, E. & Gatignon, H. Modes of Foreign Entry: A Transaction Cost Analysis and Propositions. *Journal of International Business Studies*, p. 1–26, 1986.

Anderson, E. & Weitz B. A. Make-or-Buy Decisions: Vertical Integration and Marketing Productivity. *Sloan Management Review*, p. 3–19, Spring 1986.

Anderson, E. & Weitz, B. A. The Use of Pledges to Build and Sustain Commitment in Distribution Channels. *Journal of Marketing Research,* v. 24, p. 18–34, 1992.

Anderson, J. C.; Hakansson, H. & Johanson, J. Dyadic Business Relationship Within a Business Network Context. *Journal of Marketing*, v. 58, p. 22–38, October 1994.

Anderson, J. C. & Narus, J. A. A Model of Distributor Firm and Manufacturer Firm Working Partnerships. *Journal of Marketing*, v. 54, p. 42–58, January 1990.

Araujo, L. & Mousas, S. Competition and Cooperation in Vertical Marketing Systems. In: Gemunden, H. G. et al: *Relationships and Networks in International Markets*. Elsevier: London, p. 145–165, 1997.

Atkinsons, T. & Higgins T. L. Evaluation Obstacles and Opportunities. *Forum Issues Special Report*, February 1988.

Azevedo, P. F. Integração Vertical e Barganha. Doctoral thesis, Depto. de Economia, FEA/USP, 1996.

Ballou, R. H. *Gerenciamento da Cadeia de Suprimentos*. Porto Alegre: Bookman, 2001.

Bamford, J.; Ernst, D. & Fubini, D. G. Launching a Word Class Joint Venture. *Harvard Business Review*, Online Version. February 2004.

Barkema, H. G.; Shenkar, O.; Vermeulen, F. & Bell, J.H. Working Abroad, Working With Others—How Firms Learn to Operate International Joint-Ventures. *Academy of Management Journal*, v. 40, n. 2, p. 426–442, 1997.

Bello, D. C. & Lohtia, R. Export Channel Design: The Use of Foreign Distributors and Agents. *Journal of Academy of Marketing Science*, v. 23, n. 2, p. 83–93, 1995.

Bengtson, A.; Havila, V. & Aberg, S. Business Relationships that Survive Project Termination: The Role of Product Specificity, *Proceedings from the 30th European Marketing Academy (EMAC) Conference*, Bergen, Norway, May 8–11, 2001.

Berman, B. *Marketing Channels*. Chichester: John Wiley & Sons, 1996.

Berry, L. Relationship Marketing. In: L. Berry (ed.) *Emerging Perspectives in Services Marketing*. Chicago: AMA, p. 25–28, 1983.

Berry, L. L. & Parasuraman, A. *Marketing Services: Competing Through Quality*. New York: The Free Press, 1991.

Bertalanffy, L. V. *General System Theory. Foundations, Development, Applications*. New York: George Braziller, 1968.

Besanko, D.; Dranove, D. & Shanley, M. *Economics of Strategy*. 2nd ed. New York: John Wiley & Sons, 2000.

Biong, H. et al. Why Do Some Companies Not Want to Engage in Partnering Relationships? In Gemunden, H. G. et al: *Relationships and Networks in International Markets*. London: Elsevier Science, p. 91–107, 1997.

Blois, K. J. When is a Relationship a "Relationship"?: in Gemunden, H. G., Ritter, T., Walter, A. (Eds.): *Relationships and Networks in International Markets*. London: Elsevier Science, p. 53–64, 1997.

Bonoma, T. V. Case Research in Marketing: Opportunities, Problems and a Process. *Journal of Marketing Research*, v. XXII, p. 199–208, May 1985.

Bower, L. J. Not all M&As are Alike—And That Matters. *Harvard Business Review*, v. 79, n. 3, March 1999.

Bresser, R. K. Matching Collective and Competitive Strategies. *Strategic Management Journal*, v. 9, p. 375–385, 1988.

Bridgewater, S. & Egan, C. *International Marketing Relationships*. New York: Palgrave/MacMillan, 2002.

Brown J. R. & Day R. L. Measures of Manifest Conflict in Distribution Channels. *Journal of Marketing Research*, v. XVIII, p. 263–274, August 1981.

Brown, J. R & Johnson, K. Measuring the Sources of Marketing Channel Power: A Comparison of Alternative Approaches. *International Journal of Research in Marketing*, v. 12, p. 333–354, 1995.

Bucklin, L. P. Postponement, Speculation and the Structure of Distribution Channels. *Journal of Marketing Research*, v. 2, n. 1, p. 26–31, February 1965.

Bucklin, L. P. A *Theory of Distribution Channel Structure*. Berkeley, CA: University of Berkeley Press, 1966.

Bucklin, L. P. A Theory of Channel Control. *Journal of Marketing*, v. 37, n. 1, p. 39–47, January 1973.

Bucklin, L. P.; Ramaswamy, V. & Majumdar, S. K. Analyzing Channel Structures of Business Markets via the Structure-Output Paradigm. *International Journal of Research in Marketing*, v. 13, n. 1, p. 73–87, 1996.

Bucklin, L. P. & Sengupta, S. Organizing Successful Co-Marketing Alliances. *Journal of Marketing Research*, v. 57 n. 2, p. 32–46, 1993.

Campomar, M. C. Revisando um Modelo de Plano de Marketing. *Marketing, São Paulo*, v. 17, n. 121, p. 44–47, 1983.

Camps, T. et al. *The Emerging World of Chains and Networks: Bridging Theory and Practice*. New York: Reed Business Information, 2004.

Castro, L. T. & Neves, M. F. Innovative Sales Planning and Management: A Framework Proposition. *Journal of Innovative Marketing*, v. 3, n. 2, pp. 7–17, 2007.

Chonko, L. B.; Enis B. M. & Tanner, J. F. *Managing Salespeople*. Boston, MA: Allyn and Bacon, 1992.

Christopher, M. G. *Logistics and Supply Chain Management: Srategies for Reducing Costs and Improving Services*. Pitman Publishing: London, 1998.

Christy, D. P. & Grout, J. R. Safeguarding Supply Chain Relationships. *International Journal of Production Economics*, v. 36, p. 233–242, 1994.

Churchill, A. G.; Ford, N.M.; Walker O. C., Johnston M. W. & Tanner J. F. *Sales Force Management*, 6th edition. Boston, MA: McGraw-Hill, 2000.

Claro, D. P. *Managing Business Network And Buyer-Supplier Relationships*. Veenendaal, Netherlands: Universal Press, 2004.

Claro, D. P.; Hagelaar, R. & Omta, O. The Determinants of Relational Governance and Performance: How to Manage Business Relationships? *Industrial Marketing and Management*, v. 32, n. 8, p. 703–716, 2003.

Coase, R. The Nature of the Firm. *Economica*, n.s., 4, 1937.

Coase, R. The New Institutional Economics. *American Economic Review*, v. 88, n. 2, p. 72–75, May 1998.

Cobra, M. *Administração de Vendas*. São Paulo: Atlas, 1994.

Collis, D. J. & Montgomery, C. A. Competing on Resources: Strategy in the 1990s. *Harvard Business Review*, p. 118–128, July–August 1995.

Consoli, M. A & Neves, M. F. A Method for Building New Marketing Channels: The Case of "Door-To Door" in Dairy Products. *Direct Marketing, an International Journal*, v. 2, n. 3, p. 174–185, 2008.

Cooper, J. & Lane, P. *Practical Marketing Planning*, London: MacMillan Business, 1997.

Corbett, C. J.; Blackburn, J. D. & van Wassenhove, L. N. Case Study: Partnerships to Improve Supply Chains. *Sloan Management Review*, p. 71–82, Summer 1999.

Corey, E. R.; Cespedes, F. V. & Rangan, V. K. *Going to Market—Distribution Systems for Industrial Products*. Cambridge, MA: Harvard Business School Press, 1989.

Coughlan, A. T. et al. *Canais de Marketing e Distribuição*. 6th edn. Porto Alegre: Bookman, p.461, 2002.

Coughlan, A.; Anderson, E; Stern, L. & El-Ansary, A. *Marketing Channels*. New York: Prentice Hall, 2001.

Coyle, J. J.; Bardi, E. J. & Langley, C. J. Jr. *The Management of Business Logistics : A Supply Chain Perspective*. 7th ed. Mason: Thomson Learning, 2003.

Cravens, D. W. The Changing Role of the Sales Force. *Marketing Management*, v. 4, n. 2, p. 49–57, Fall 1995.

Crescitelli, E. *Marketing de Incentivos*. São Paulo: Cobra, 2002.

Czinkota, M. R. *Marketing: As Melhores Práticas*. Porto Alegre: Bookman, 2001.

Dalrymple, D. J. & Cron, W. L. *Sales Management: Concepts and Cases*. New York: John Wiley & Sons, 5th. ed, 1995.

Davidson, W. R. Changes in the Distributive Institutions. *Journal of Marketing*, v. 34 n. 1, p. 7–10, January 1970.

Dawes, P. & Massey, G. Relationships Between Marketing & Sales: The Role of Power and Influence. *Proceedings of the 17th Industrial Marketing and Purchasing Group Conference*, Oslo, Norway, 2001.

Dnes, A. W. The Economic Analysis of Franchise Contracts. *Journal of Institutional and Theoretical Economics*, v. 152, p. 297–324, 1996.

Dommermuth, W. & Andersen, R. C. Distribution Systems: Firms, Functions and Efficiencies. *MSU Business Topics*, p. 51–56, 1969.

Doney, P. M. & Cannon, J. P. An Examination of the Nature of Trust in Buyer-Seller Relationships. *Journal of Marketing*, v. 61, p. 35–51, April 1997.

Dubinsky, A. J. & Hansen, R. W. The Salesforce Management Audit. *California Management Review*, v. XXIV, n. 2, p. 86–95, Winter 1981.

Dwyer, F. R. & Oh, S. A Transaction Cost Perspective on Vertical Integration Structure and Interchannel Competitive Strategies. *Journal of Marketing*, v. 52, p. 21–34, 1998.

Dwyer, F. R.; Schurr, P. H. & Oh, S. Developing Buyer-Seller Relationships. *Journal of Marketing*, v. 51, p.11–27, April 1987.

Dwyer, S.; Hill, J. & Martin, W. An Empirical Investigation of Critical Success Factors in the Personal Selling Process for Homogeneus Goods. *Journal of Personal Selling & Sales Management*, v. XX, n. 3, p. 151–159, Summer 2000.

Dyer, J. H. Effective Inter-Firm Collaboration: How Firms Minimize Transaction Costs and Maximize Transaction Value. *Strategic Management Journal*, v. 18, n. 7, p. 535–556, 1997.

Dyer, J. H.; Kale, P., & Singh, H. How to Make Strategic Alliances Work. *Sloan Management Review*, v. 42, no. 4, p. 37–43, Summer 2001.

Eisenhardt, K. M. Building theory From Case Study Research. *Academy of Management Review*, v. 14, n. 4, p. 532–550, 1989.

Eisenhardt, K. M. & Martin, J.A. Dynamic Capabilities: What are They? *Strategic Management Journal*, v. 21, p. 1105–1121, 2000.

El-Ansary, A. I. & Stern, L. W. Power Measurement in the Distribution Channel. *Journal of Marketing Research*, v. 9, p. 47–52, 1972.

Ellis, P. International Trade Intermediaries and the Development of Local Marketing, *Proceedings from the 30th European Marketing Academy (EMAC) Conference*, Bergen, Norway, May 8–11, 2001.

Engel, J. F.; Blackwell, R. D. & Miniard, P. W. *Consumer Behavior*. New York: Dryden, 1995.

Etzel, M. J.; Walker, B. J. & Stanton, W. J. *Marketing*. São Paulo: Makron Books, 2001.

Farina, E. M.; Azevedo P. F. & Saes, M. S. M. *Competitividade: Mercado, Estado e Organizações*. São Paulo: Singular, 1997.

Ford, D. Two Decades of Interaction, Relationships and Networks. In: Naudé, P. & Turnbull, P. W. (Eds.): *Network Dynamics in International Marketing*. Oxford: Pergamon International Business and Management, p. 3–15, 1998.

Ford, D.; Gadde, L.; Hakansson, H. & Snehota, I. Managing Networks. *Proceedings of the 18th Industrial Marketing and Purchasing Group Conference*, Dijon, France, 2002.

Frazier, G. L. & Summers, J. O. Interfirm Influence Strategies and Their Application Within Distribution Channels. *Journal of Marketing*, v. 48, p. 43–55, 1984.

Friedman, L. G. & Furey, T. R. *The Channel Advantage*. London: Butterworth Heinemann, 1999.

Futrell, C. *Vendas: Fundamentos e Novas Práticas de Gestão*. São Paulo: Saraiva, 2003.

Gadde, L. E. & Hakansson, H. *Supply Network Strategies*. New York: John Wiley & Sons, 2001.

Ganesan, S. Determinants of Long-Term Orientation in Buyer-Seller Relationships. *Journal of Marketing*, v. 58, p. 1–19, April 1994.

Gaski, J. F. The Theory of Power and Conflict in Channels of Distribution. *Journal of Marketing*, v. 48, n. 3, p. 9–29, Summer 1984.

Gattorna, J. L. & Walters, D.W. *Managing the Supply Chain*, New York: MacMillan, p. 189–203, 1996.

Gemunden, H. G. *Relationships and Networks In International Markets*. Oxford: Pergamon, 1997.

Gemunden, H. G. & Ritter, T. Managing Technological Networks: The Concept of Network Competence. In: Gemunden, H. G. et al: *Relationships and Networks in International Markets*. Oxford: Pergamon, p. 294–304, 1997.

Georges, L; Guenzi, P. & Pardo C. The Link Between the Supplier's Relational Strategy and Its Key Account Managers' Relational Behaviours. *Proceedings of the 18th Industrial Marketing and Purchasing Group Conference*, Dijon, France, 2002.

Geysks, I.; Steenkamp J. E. M. & Kumar N. A Meta-Analysis of Satisfaction in Marketing Channel Relationships. *Journal of Marketing Research*, v. XXXVI, p. 223–238, May 1999.

Ghemawat, P. Commitment: *The Dynamic of Strategy*. New York: Free Press, 1991.

Gilligan, C. & Wilson, R. M. S. *Strategic Marketing Planning*, London: Butterworth-Heinemann, 2002.

Grant, R. M. *Contemporary Strategy Analysis: Concepts, Techniques and Applications*. 4th ed. Oxford: Blackwell, 2002.

Gray, A.; Boehlje, M. & Akridge, J. Strategic Positioning in Agribusiness: Analysis and Options, Working Papers 04–13, Purdue University, Department of Agricultural Economics, September 2004.

Gulati, R. Alliances and Networks. *Strategic Management Journal*, v. 19, p. 293–317, 1998.

Hahn, M. & Chang, D. R. An Extended Framework for Adjusting Channel Strategies in Industrial Markets. *The Journal of Business & Industrial Marketing*, v. 7, n. 2, p. 31–43, Spring 1992.

Hair, J. F. Jr.; Anderson, R. E.; Tatham, R. L. & Black, W. C. *Multivariate Data Analysis with Readings*. 4th edition. New York: Prentice Hall, 1995.

Hakansson, H. & Persson, G. Supply Chain Management: The Logic of Supply Chains and Networks. *The International Journal of Logistics Management*, v. 15, n. 1, p. 11–26, 2004.

Hakansson, H. & Snehota, I. The Burden of Relationships: Who is Next? In: Naudé, P. & Turnbull, P. W. (Eds.): *Network Dynamics in International Marketing*. Oxford: Pergamon, p. 16–25, 1998.

Harper, P. Merging Cultures. *Executive Excellence*, v. 19, n. 11, p. 12, 2002.

Heide, J. B. Interorganizational Governance in Marketing Channels. *Journal of Marketing*, v. 58, p. 71–85, January 1994.

Heide, J. B. & John, G. The Role of Dependence Balancing in Safeguarding Transaction. Specific Assets in Conventional Channels. *Journal of Marketing*, v. 52, p. 20–35, 1988.

Heide, J. B. & John, G. Alliances in Industrial Purchasing: The Determinants of Joint Action in Buyer-Supplier Relationships. *Journal of Marketing Research*, v. 27, p. 24–36, 1990.

Heide, J. B. & John, G. Do Norms Matter in Marketing Relationships? *Journal of Marketing*, v. 56, p. 32–44, 1992.

Heide, J. B. & Miner, A. S. The Shadow of the Future: Effects of Anticipated Interaction and Frequency of Contact on Buyer-Seller Cooperation. *Academy of Management Journal*, v. 35, n. 2, p. 265–291, 1992.

Hertz, S. & Mattsson, L. Dynamics of Contemporary International Markets-Strategic Alliances and Reconfiguration of Network Structures. *Proceedings from the 30th European Marketing Academy (EMAC) Conference, Bergen,* Norway, May 8–11, 2001.

Heschel, M. S. Effective Sales Territory Development. *Journal of Marketing*, p. 39–43, April 1977.

Heydebreck, P. & Maier, J. C. Need Bundles of Innovation-oriented Services and Resources. In Gemunden, H.G. et al.: *Relationships and Networks in International Markets.* Oxford: Pergamon, 1997: p. 427–444.

Hobbs, J. E. A Transaction Cost Approach to Supply Chain Management. *Supply Chain Management*, v. 1, n. 2, p. 15–27, 1996.

Honeycutt, E. D. Sales Management in the New Millennium: An Introduction. *Industrial Marketing Management*, v. 31, p. 555–558, 2002.

Hunt, S. D. & Nevin, J. R. Power in a Channel of Distribution: Sources and Consequences. *Journal of Marketing Research*, v. 11, p. 186–193, 1974.

Hutt, M. & Speh, T. *B2B: Gestão de Marketing em Mercados Industriais e Organizacionais.* Porto Alegre: Bookman, 2002.

Ingenbleek, P.; Verhallen, T. M. M.; Debruyne, M. & Frambach, R. T. Effective Pricing of New Products in a Competitive Context. *Proceedings from the 30th European Marketing Academy (EMAC) Conference,* Bergen, Norway, May 8–11, 2001.

Ingram, T. N. & Bellenger, D. N. Motivational Segments in the Sales Force. *California Management Review*, v. XXIV, n. 3, p. 81–88, Spring 1982.

Ingram, T. N. & Laforge, R. W. *Sales Management – Analysis and Decision Making*, 2nd edition. Orlando: HBJ, 1992.

Ingram, T. N.; LaForge, R. W. & Leigh T. W. Selling in the New Millennium: A Joint Agenda. *Industrial Marketing Management*, v. 31, p. 559–567, 2002.

Inkpen, A. C. & Beamish, P. W. Knowledge, Bargaining Power and Instability of International Joint-Ventures. The *Academy of Management Review*, v. 22, n. 1, p. 177–202, 1997.

Jackson, D. M. & d'Amico, M. F. Products and Markets Served by Distributors and Agents. *Industrial Marketing Management*, v. 18, p. 27–33, 1989.

Jain, S. C. *Marketing Planning & Strategy*, 6th edition. Cincinnati, OH: Thomson Learning, 2000.

Jobber, D. & Lancaster, G. *Selling and Sales Management.* London: Prentice Hall, 2000.

John, G. An Empirical Investigation of Some Antecedents of Opportunism in a Marketing Channel. *Journal of Marketing Research*, v. 21, p. 278–289, August 1984.

Johnson, G. & Scholes, K. *Exploring Corporate Strategy*, 4th. edition. New York: Prentice Hall, 1997.

Jorgensen, S. & Zaccour, G. Channel Coordination Over Time: Incentive Equilibrium and Credibility. *Journal of Economic Dynamics & Control*, v. 27, n. 1, p. 801–822, 2003.

Kemp, R. G. M. *Managing Interdependence for Joint Venture Success: An Empirical Study of Dutch International Joint Ventures*. Groningen: Groningen Press, 1999.

Klein, B. Contracts and Incentives: The Role of Contract Terms in Assuring Performance. In: Werin, L. & Wijkander, H.: *Contract Economics*. London: Blackwell Publishers, 1992: p. 149–171.

Klein, B. The Economics of Franchise Contracts. *Journal of Corporate Finance*, v. 2, p. 9–37, 1995.

Klein, J. A. & Hiscocks, P. G. Competence-Based Competition: A Practical Toolkit. In: Hamel, G. & Heene, A. (eds.): *Competence-Based Competition*. Chichester: John Wiley & Sons, p. 183–212., 1994.

Klein. S.; Frazier, G. L. & Roth, V. J. A Transactional Cost Analysis Model of Channel Integration in International Markets. *Journal of Marketing Research*, v. 27, p. 196–208, May 1990.

Kogut, B. Joint Ventures: Theoretical and Empirical Perspectives. *Strategic Management Journal*, v. 9, n. 4, p. 319–332, 1990.

Kotler, P. A Generic Concept of Marketing. *Journal of Marketing*, v. 36, p. 46–54, April 1972.

Kotler, P. *Administração de Marketing*. 10th edition. New York: Prentice Hall, 2000.

Kozak, R. A. & Cohen, D. H. Distributor-Supplier Partnering Relationships: A Case in Trust. *Journal of Business Research*, v. 39, p. 33–38, 1997.

Lafontaine, F. & Masten, S. E. Franchise Contracting, Organization and Regulation: Introduction. *Journal of Corporate Finance*, v. 2, p. 1–7, 1995.

Lambert, D. M. & Cooper, M. C. Issues in Supply Chain Management. *Industrial Marketing Management*, v.29, p.65–83, 2000.

Lambin, J. J. *Marketing Estratégico*, 4th edition. Lisbon: McGraw-Hill, 2000.

Las Casas, A. L. *Plano de Marketing para Micro e Pequena Empresa*. São Paulo: Editora Atlas, 1999.

Lazzarini, S. G.; Chaddad, F. R. & Cook, M. Integrating Supply and Network Analysis: The Study of Netchains. *Journal on Chain and Network Science*, v. 1, n. 1, p. 7–22, 2001.

Levitt, T. After the Sale is Over. *Harvard Business Review*, v. 61, n. 5, p. 87–93, 1983.

Lewis, E. H. *Marketing Channels: Structure and Strategy*. New York: McGraw-Hill, 1968.

Lindgreen, A. A Framework for Studying Relationship Marketing Dyads. *Qualitative Marketing Research*, v. 4, n. 2, p.75–88, 2001.

Löning, H. & Besson, M. Can Distribution Channels Explain Differences in Marketing and Sales Performance Measurement Systems? *European Management Journal*, v. 20, n. 6, p. 597–609, 2002.

Lorange, P.; Roos, J. & Bronn, P. S. Building Successful Strategic Alliances. *Long Range Planning*, v. 25, n. 6, p. 10–17, 1992.

Lusch, R. F. Sources of Power: Their Impact on Intrachannel Conflict. *Journal of Marketing Research*, v. 13, p. 382–390, 1976.

Lusch, R. F. & Brown J. R. Interdependency, Contracting and Relational Behaviour in Marketing Channels. *Journal of Marketing*, v. 60, p. 19–38, October 1996.

Lynch, R. P. *Business Alliance Guide*. Chichester: John Willey & Sons, 1993.

Mahoney, J. T. & Pandian, R. J. The Resource-Based View Within the Conversation of Strategic Management. *Strategic Management Journal*, v. 13, p. 363–380, 1992.

Malhotra, N. K. *Marketing Research: An Applied Orientation*, 2nd edition. New York: Prentice Hall, 1996.

Malhotra, N. *Pesquisa de Marketing*. Porto Alegre: Bookman, 2001.

Martinelli, D. P. & Almeida, A. P. *Negociação: Como Transformar Conflito em Cooperação*. São Paulo: Atlas, 1997.

Martinelli, D. P. *Negociação e Solução de Conflitos: Do Impasse ao Ganha-Ganha Através do Melhor Estilo*. São Paulo: Atlas, 1998.

Mattsson, L. "Relationship Marketing" in a Network Perspective. In: Gemunden, H. G., Ritter, T. & Walter, A. (Eds.): *Relationships and Networks in International Markets*. Oxford: Pergamon, p. 37–47, 1997.

McCalley, R. W. *Marketing Channel Management: People, Products, Programs and Markets*. Danbury, CT: Praeger, 1996.

McDonald, M. *Marketing Plans: How to Prepare Them, How to Use Them*. Oxford: Butterworth Heinemann, 2002.

Mehta, R.; Dubinsky, A. I. & Anderson, R. E. Marketing Channel Management and the Sales Manager. *Industrial Marketing Management*, v. 31, p. 429–439, 2002.

Ménard, C. Methodological Issues in New Institutional Economics. *Journal of Economic Methodology*, v. 8, n. 1, p. 85–92, 2001.

Mintzberg, H. *The Rise and Fall of Strategic Planning*. New York: Prentice Hall, 1994.

Mitchell, W. & Singh, K. Survival of Business Using Collaborative Relationships to Commercialize Complex Goods. *Strategic Management Journal*, v. 17, n. 3, p. 169–195, 1996.

Mohr, J. & Spekman, R. Characteristics of Partnership Success: Partnership Attributes, Communication Behavior and Conflict Resolution Techniques. *Strategic Management Journal*, v. 15, n. 2, p. 135–152, 1994.

Monczka, R.; Trent, R. & Handfield, R. *Purchasing and Supply Chain Management*. 2nd edition. Cinccinati, OH: Thomson Learning, 2002.

Morgan, R. M. & Hunt, S. D. The Commitment-Trust Theory of Relationship Marketing. *Journal of Marketing*, v. 58, p. 20–38, July 1994.

Mowery, D. C.; Oxley, J. E. & Silverman, B. S. Strategic Alliances and Interfirm Knowledge Transfer. *Strategic Management Journal*, v. 17, p. 77–91, 1996.

Naudé, P. & Turnbull, P. W. *Network Dynamics in International Marketing*. Oxford: Pergamon, 1998.

Neves, M. F. Marketing and Network Contracts (Agreements). *Journal of Chain and Network Science*, v. 3, n. 1, May 2003.

Neves, M. F. Strategic Marketing Plans and Collaborative Networks. *Marketing Intelligence and Planning*, v. 25, n. 2, p. 175–192, 2007.

Neves, M. F. et al. Building Joint Ventures in Six Steps: A South American Case. *Journal of Problems and Perspectives in Management*, v. 4, n. 4, p. 12–25, 2006.

Neves, M. F. & Scare, R.F. *Marketing & Exportação*. São Paulo: Atlas, 2001.

Neves, M. F.; Zuurbier, P. & Campomar, M. C. A Model for the Distribution Channels Planning Process, *Journal of Business and Industrial Marketing*, v. 16, n. 7, p. 518–540, 2001.

Nielsen, R. P. Cooperative Strategy. *Strategic Management Journal*, v. 9, p. 475–492, 1988.

Noonan, C. *Chartered Institute of Marketing Handbook of Export Marketing*, 2nd edition. Oxford: Butterworth-Heinemann, 1999.

Oksanen, E. Organizational Roles of Sales People in the Network Marketing Context. *Proceedings of the 16th Industrial Marketing and Purchasing Group Conference*, Bath, UK, 2000.

Olson, E. M.; Cravens, D. W. & Slater, S. F. Competitiveness and Sales Management: A Marriage of Strategies. *Business Horizons*, p. 25–30, March–April 2001.

Olson, M. *Lógica da Ação Coletiva*. São Paulo: Edusp, 1st. edition, 1999.

Omta, S. W. F.; Trienekens, J. H. & Beers, G. Chain and Network Science: A Research Framework. *Journal of Chain and Network Science*, v. 1, n. 1, p.1-6, 2001.

Osborn, R. N. & Baughn, C. C. Forms of Interorganizational Governance for Multinational Alliances. *Academy of Management Journal*, v. 40, p. 261-287, 1997.

Park, S. H. & Ungson, G. R. The Effect of National Culture, Organizational Complementarity and Economic Motivation of Joint Venture Dissolution. *Academy of Management Journal*, v. 40, n. 2, p. 279-307, 1997.

Pearce, R. J. Toward Understanding Joint Venture Performance and Survival: A Bargaining and Influence Approach to Transaction Cost Theory. *The Academy of Management Review*, v. 22, n. 1, p. 203-225, 1997.

Pelton, L. E.; Strutton, D. & Lumpkin, J. R. *Marketing Channels: A Relationship Management Approach*. Boston, MA: McGraw-Hill, 1997.

Phillips, L. W. Explaining Control Losses in Corporate Marketing Channels: An Organizational Analysis. *Journal of Marketing Research*, v. 19, p. 525-548, November 1982.

Piercy, N. F.; Cravens, D. W. & Morgan, N.A. Relationships Between Sales Management Control, Territory Design, Salesforce Performance and Sales Organization Effectiveness. *British Journal of Management*, v. 10, p. 95-111, 1999.

Porter, M. *Competitive Strategy*. New York: The Free Press, 1980.

Powell, W. W. Neither Market Nor Hierarchy: Network Forms of Organization. *Research in Organizational Behavior*, v. 12, p.295-336, 1990.

Prahalad, C. K. & Hamel, G. The Core Competences of the Corporation. *Harvard Business Review*, p. 79-91, May-June 1990.

Purohit, D. & Staelin, R. Rentals, Sales, and Buybacks: Managing Secondary Distribution Channels. *Journal of Marketing Research*, v. XXXI, p. 325-338, August 1994.

Rangan, V. K.; Menezes, M. A. J. & Maier, E. P. Channel Selection for New Industrial Products: A Framework, Method and Application. *Journal of Marketing*, v. 56, p. 69-82, July 1992.

Rangaswamy, A.; Sinha, P. & Zoltners, A. An Integrated Model-Based Approach for Sales Force Structuring. *Marketing Science*, v. 9, n. 4, p. 279-298, Fall 1990.

Ries, A. & Trout, J. *Positioning*. New York: McGraw-Hill, 1995.

Rindfleisch, A. & Heide, J. B. Transaction Cost Analysis: Past, Present and Future Applications. *Journal of Marketing*, v. 61, p. 30-54, October 1997.

Ring, P. S. Structuring Cooperative Relationships Between Organizations. *Strategic Management Journal*, v. 13, p. 483-498, 1992.

Ring, P. S. & van de Ven, A. H. Developmental Processes of Cooperative Interorganizational Relationships. *Academy of Management Review*, v. 19, p. 90-118, 1994.

Robinson, P. J.; Faris C. W. & Wind, Y. *Industrial Buying and Creative Marketing*. Boston: Allyn & Bacon, 1967.

Rogers, L. *Administração de Vendas e Marketing*. São Paulo: Makron Books, 1993.

Rosenbloom, B. Conflict and Channel Efficiency: Some Conceptual Models for the Decision Maker. *Journal of Marketing*, v. 37, p. 28, July 1973.

Rosenbloom, B. *Marketing Channels,* 6th edition. New York: Dryden Press, 1999.

Ross, B. & Turnbull, P. W. The Process of Adaptation in Inter-Firm Relationship. In: Gemunden, H. G. et al: *Relationships and Networks in International Markets*. Oxford: Pergamon, p. 65-80, 1997,

Rossi, R. M.; Neves, M. F. & Tornavoi, D. Características do processo de decisão de compra de citricultores paulistas em relação a fertilizantes foliar. *Anais do 41º*

Congresso da Sober. Sociedade Brasileira de Economia Rural. Juiz de Fora, M.G., July 2003.

Rubio, A. G. & Redondo, Y. P. The Impact of Launch Strategies on New Product Success. *Proceedings from the 30th European Marketing Academy (EMAC) Conference,* Bergen, Norway, May 8–11, 2001.

Ruekert, R. W. & Churchill, G. A. Reliability and Validity of Alternative Measures of Channel Member Satisfaction. *Journal of Marketing Research,* v. 21, n. 2, p. 226–233, May 1984.

Ryans, A. B. & Weinberg, C. B. Sales Force Management: Integrating Research Advances. *California Management Review,* v. 24, n. 1, p. 75–89, 1981.

Ryans, A. B. & Weinberg, C. B. Territory response sales models: stability over time. *Journal of Marketing Research,* v. 24, p. 229–233, May 1987.

Sauvee, L. Efficiency, Effectiveness and the Design of Network Governance. 5th. International Conference on Chain Management in Agribusiness and the Food Industry, Netherlands, 2002.

Schwartz, A. Legal Contract Theories and Incomplete Contracts. In: Werin, L. & Wijkander, H.: *Contract Economics.* London: Blackwell Publishers, p. 76–109, 1992.

Semenick, R. J. & Bamossy, G. J. *Princípios de Marketing: Uma Perspectiva Global.* São Paulo: Makron Books, 1995.

Shapiro, B. et al. *Conquistando Clientes.* São Paulo: Makron Books, 1995.

Sheth, J. N.; Mittal, B. & Newman, B. I. *Comportamento do Cliente: Indo Além do Comportamento do Consumidor.* Tradução: Lenita M. R. Esteves. São Paulo: Atlas, 2001.

Sinha, P. & Zoltners, A. A. Sales-Force Decision Models: Insights from 25 Years of Implementation. *Interfaces,* v. 31, May–June 2001.

Slack, N.; Chambers, S. & Johnston, R. *Operations Management.* New York: Prentice Hall, 2001.

Slone, R. E.; Mentzer, J. T. & Dittmann, J. P. Are You the Weakest Link in Your Company's Supply Chain? *Harvard Business Review,* v. 85, n. 9, p. 116–127, 2007.

Smit, W.; Bruggen, G. H. & Wierenga, B. Will Information Sharing lead to Better Marketing Channel Relationships: Findings from a Laboratory Experiment. *Proceedings from the 30th European Marketing Academy (EMAC) Conference, Bergen,* Norway, May 8–11, 2001.

Sonnenberg, F. K. Partnering: Entering the Age of Cooperation. *Journal of Business Strategy,* v. 13, p. 49–52, May–June 1992.

Souza, R. F. Canais de Marketing, Valor e Estruturas de Governança. RAE. *Revista de Administração de Empresas,* v. 42, n. 2, p. 42–53, 2002.

Spekman, R. E.; Forbes, T. M.; Isabella, L. A. & Macavoy, T. C. Alliance Management: A View From the Past and a Look to the Future. *Journal of Management Studies,* v. 35, p. 791–811, 2000.

Spens, K. M. & Bask, A. H. Developing a Framework for Supply Chain Management. *The International Journal of Logistics Management,* v. 13, n. 1, p. 73–88, 2002.

Stalk, G.; Evans, P. & Shulman, L. Competing Capabilities: the New Rules of Corporate Strategy. *Harvard Business Review,* p. 57–69, March/April 1992.

Stern, L.; El-Ansary, A. I. & Coughlan, A. *Marketing Channels,* 5th edition. New York: Prentice Hall, 1996.

Stevens, G. Integrating the Supply Chain. *International Journal of Physical Distribution & Materials Management,* v.19, n. 8, p.3–8, 2001.

Stiglitz, J. E. Contract Theory and Macroeconomic Fluctuations. In: Werin, L. & Wijkander, H.: *Contract Economics*. London: Blackwell, p. 293–322, 1992.

Svensson, G. The Theoretical Foundation of Supply Chain Management: A Functionalist Theory of Marketing. *The International Journal of Physical Distribution & Logistics*, v. 32, n. 9, p. 734–754, 2002.

Tanner J. F. & Dudley, G. W. Why Do Salespeople Sell. *Baylor Business Review*, v. 21, n. 11, p. 44–46, 2003.

Tirole, J. Comments on the Paper of Schwart. In: Werin, L. & Wijkander, H.: *Contract Economics*. London: Blackwell, p. 109–113, 1992.

Tosun, N. Industrial Marketing and Communications Strategies. *Proceedings of the 19th Industrial Marketing and Purchasing Group Conference*, Lugano, Switzerland, 2003.

Trienekens, J. & Zuurbier, P. J. P. *Proceedings of the Second International Conference on Chain Management in Agribusiness and the Food Industry–Management Studies Group*. Wageningen University, Netherlands, 1996.

van der Vorst, J. *Effective Food Supply Chains: Generating, Modeling and Evaluating Supply Chain Scenarios*. Wageningen: Wageningen Press, 2000.

van der Vorst, J. G.; Beulens, A. J. M. & van Beek, P. Supply Chain Management in Food Chains: Improving Performance by Reducing Uncertainty. *International Transactions in Operational Research*, v. 5, n. 6, p. 487–499, 1998.

Webster Jr., F. E. The Changing Role of Marketing in The Corporation. *Journal of Marketing*, v. 56, p. 1–17, 1992.

Weiss, A. M. & Anderson, E. Converting from Independent to Employee Salesforces: The Role of Perceived Switching Costs. *Journal of Marketing Research*, v. 29, p. 101–115, 1992.

Weitz, B. A.; Castleberry, S. B. & Tanner, J. F. *Selling: Building Partnerships*. New York: McGraw-Hill, 2004.

Werin, L. & Wijkander, H. *Contract Economics*. London: Blackwell Publishers, 1992.

Wernerfelt, B. A Resource View of the Firm. *Strategic Management Journal*. v. 5, n. 2, p. 171–180, 1984.

Westwood, J. *Plano de Marketing*. São Paulo: Makron Books, 1995.

Wilkinson, I. A History of Network and Channels Thinking in Marketing in the 20th Century. *Australian Journal of Marketing*, v. 9, n. 2, p. 23–53, 2001.

Williamson, O. E. *The Economics Institutions of Capitalism*. New York: The Free Press, 1985.

Williamson, O. E. *The Mechanism of Governance*. Oxford: Oxford University Press, 1996.

Williamson, O. E. The New Institutional Economics: Taking Stock, Looking Ahead. *Journal of Economic Literature*, v. 38, n. 3, p. 595–620, 2000.

Wilson, E. J. & Vlosky, R. P. Partnering Relationship Activities: Building Theory from Case Study Research. *Journal of Business Research*, v. 39, p. 59–70, 1997.

Winer, L. The Effect of Product Sales Quotas on Sales Force Productivity. *Journal of Marketing Research*, v. 10, p. 180–183, May 1973.

Wood, M. B. *Marketing Planning: Principles into Practice*. Harlow: Prentice Hall, 2004.

Wright, P.; Kroll, M. K. & Parnell, J. *Administração Estratégica: Conceitos*. São Paulo: Atlas, 2000.

Yin, R. K. *Case Study Research: Design and Methods*, 2nd edition. London: Sage Publications, 1994.

Yin, R. K. *Estudo de Caso: Planejamento e Métodos*, 2nd edition. Porto Alegre: Bookman, 2001.

Zeyl, A. An Analytical Framework of selling Situations Within Relationships and Their Impact on the Role of the Sales Force. *Proceedings of the 18th Industrial Marketing and Purchasing Group Conference*, Dijon, France, 2002.

Ziggers, G. W.; Trienekens, J. & Zuurbier, P. J. P. *Proceedings of the Third International Conference on Chain Management in Agribusiness and the Food Industry*. Management Studies Group. Wageningen University, Netherlands, 1998.

Zoltners A. A. & Lorimer S. E. Sales Territory Alignment: An Overlooked Productivity Tool. *Journal of Personal Selling & Sales Management*, v. 20, n. 3, p. 139–150, 2000.

Zoltners, A. A.; Sinha, P. & Zoltners, G. A. *The Complete Guide to Accelerating Sales Force Performance*. New York: Amacom, 2001.

Zylbersztajn, D. Estruturas de Governança e Coordenação do Agribusiness: Uma aplicação da Nova Economia das Instituições. Doctoral Thesis, Departamento de Administração da Faculdade de Economia, Administração e Contabilidade da Universidade de São Paulo (FEA/USP), 1995.

Zylbersztajn, D. & Farina, E. M. Agri-System Management: Recent Developments and Applicability of the Concept. Paper presented at the First Brazilian Workshop on Agri-Chain Management, FEA/USP, Ribeirão Preto, SP, p. 18–38, November 1997.

Zylbersztajn, D. & Farina, E. Strictly Coordinated Food-Systems: Exploring the Limits of the Coasian Firm. *International Food and Agribusiness Management Review*, v. 2, n. 2, p. 249–265, 1999.

Zylbersztajn, D. & Neves, M. F. *Economia e Gestão dos Negócios Agroalimentares*. São Paulo: Pioneira, 2000.

Index

Figures are indicated by **bold** page numbers, tables by *italic* numbers.

Alderson, W. 39
Anderson, J.C. 30
asset specificity analysis *30*, 30–2, *31*, *32*, 52, 54–6, *57*, *58*
Azevedo, P.F. 52

Bello, D.C. 52
benchmarking 32
brand specificity 55
business relationships, network perspective on 5

channels: design of marketing 38–40, **40**; management of 34–5; power of 29; selection of 34
Chonko, L.B. 68
Churchill, A.G. 66
collaborative networks: Strategic Marketing Planning and Management (SMPM) Process 19, **19**, *20–1*, 22, **22**, **23**; *see also* joint ventures
collective actions by sales forces 71–2
communication flow 27
communication management 69, 76–8, **77**, *77*
communications analysis for marketing plans *20*
competition, basis of 103, *104*
competition/customer balance **17**, 17–18
competitor analysis for marketing plans *20*
competitors on the network 11–12
conflict management 69, 78
conflict sources 34

consumers 33
contracts: analysis of in networks 51–2, *53–4*, *54*, 54–6, *57*, *58*; asset specificity and risk analysis 52, 54–6, *57*, *58*; building 34; improvements to 56, 59, *59*; need for 50–1; power sources 56, *62–3*; reward mechanism 59
contractual analysis 32
control measures for sales forces 78
control sources 56, *62–3*
cooperative actions and networks 5
core competencies 84, *85*
Coughlan, A. 38, 39, 41, 47
critical success factors for joint ventures 87, *88*, 89
Cron, W.L. 68
customer/competition balance **17**, 17–18
customers 33, 103, *103*

Dalrymple, D.J. 68
Davidson, W.R. 38–9
dedicated specificity 54
demand-driven orientation: customer/competition balance **17**, 17–18; as response to market changes 17
design of marketing channels 38–40, **40**
distribution channel planning process: asset specificity analysis *30*, 30–2, *31*, *32*; building contracts and relationships 34; channel management 34–5; for competitive advantage 24; conflict sources 34; and the consumer 33; contractual analysis 32; description of chain and network 26; description of channels 27–8; environmental analysis *28*, 28–30, *29*; first and following analyses

35; flows *27, 27–8*; gap analysis 33; marketing research 33; new aspects of 25; objectives of the company 32–3; overview of phases 25–6, **26**; quick adjustments 33; selection of channels 34

distribution channels: efficiency in 41; factors contributing to change in 39; importance of 39; services production 39–40, **40**; systemic view 38–9; *see also* value creation and capture

distributions channels: for marketing plans *21*

distributors: analysis of performance 94; benefits design for incentive system 95, *98*; benefits of marketing incentives for 92; defining objectives with 94; designing incentives for **93,** 93–9, *96–8*; importance of relationship with 91–2; improvement of performance 98; instruction role of marketing incentives 98; performance measures 94–5; performance measures for *96–7*

economic environment 28
efficiency in distribution channels 41
El-Ansary, A.I. 38
employment status of salespeople 70–1, 75–6, *76*
environmental analysis *20, 28,* 28–30, *29*
external trends and the network 14

facilitators of the network 11
financial flows 28
flows *27, 27–8*; responsibilities in contracts 52, *53–4*; services production by 39, **40**
focal company: designing marketing channels 9–11, **10**; designing the supply chain 8–9, **9**

gap analysis 33
Gattorna, J.L. 33
goals of the company 32–3
Grant, R.M. 102, 103
Gulati, R. 82, 87

incentives, marketing: analysis of distributors' performance 94; benefits design 95, *98*; benefits of using with distributors 92; defining objectives with distributors 94; designing for distributors **93,** 93–9, *96–8*;

implementation of 98; instruction role of 98; performance measures for distributors 94–5, *96–7*

information and communication management 69, 76–8, *77,* **77**
information flow 28
Ingram, T.N. 66
instruction role of marketing incentives 98
intensification of marketing channels 9–10

John, G. 30
joint ventures: advantages of 86, *87;* alternative arrangements 86; core competencies 84, *85;* critical success factors for 87, *88,* 89; defined 80; framework for building 81–9, **82,** *83–8;* launching 89; managers in 89; market analysis for 83–4, *84;* and networks 5; objectives of each participant 85, *86;* relationship history 81–3, *83*

key success factors: analysing *105,* 105–7, **106,** *107;* identifying **102,** 102–5, *103–5;* and strategy *108–9;* use of as tool 101–2

Laforge, R.W. 66
legal environment 28–9
local specificity 55
Lumpkin, J.R. 41
Lynch, R.P. 34

market changes 16–17
marketing channels 7, 8, 9–11, **10;** design of 38–40, **40;** intensification of 9–10
marketing flows 7–8, 11, *12;* responsibilities in contracts 52, *53–4;* services production by 39, **40**
marketing incentives: analysis of distributors' performance 94, *96–8;* benefits design *98;* benefits of using with distributors 92; defining objectives with distributors 94; designing for distributors **93;** implementation of 98; instruction role of 98; performance measures for distributors 94–5, *96–7*
marketing plans: demand-driven orientation **17,** 17–18; strategic and operational management 18, **18;** Strategic Marketing Planning and